Charles M. Taylor

The British Isles Through an Opera Glass

Charles M. Taylor

The British Isles Through an Opera Glass

ISBN/EAN: 9783337213114

Printed in Europe, USA, Canada, Australia, Japan

Cover: Foto ©Thomas Meinert / pixelio.de

More available books at **www.hansebooks.com**

The British Isles
Through an Opera Glass

By CHARLES M. TAYLOR, Jr.

Fellow of The Royal Geographical Society and of the American Geographical Society

Author of "Vacation Days in Hawaii and Japan"

With Map and Forty-eight Illustrations

Philadelphia

GEORGE W. JACOBS & CO.

1899

To my dear Mother
This volume is affectionately inscribed

CONTENTS

	PAGE
ABROAD—PARIS—"MERRIE ENGLAND."	9

Sail for Havre—Paris—Champs Elysées—Bois de Boulogne—St. Cloud—The Louvre—Tuileries—Place de la Concorde — Versailles — Père la Chaise—London—The Thames—Richmond Hill—Hyde Park—The Tower—British Museum—Westminster Abbey—South Kensington Museum—London Bridge—Hampton Court—Kew Gardens—Planning a Tour—Ireland, Scotland and the English Lakes—London Street Cries—Living Expenses at Home and Abroad—We Leave London—Travelling Companions—Liverpool—A Bank Holiday—New Brighton—" Salvationists "—Parliament.

DUBLIN—BRAY—PICTURESQUE IRELAND	37

En Route for Dublin—Holyhead—Kingstown—Dublin—An Irish Jaunting Car—Petticoat Lane—Sackville Street—Hill of Howth—Bray—Enniskerry — Glen of the Downs — Esplanade— A Little Irish Boy — Sketching Bray Head — Spectators—Sugar Loaf Mountain—Rathdrum—The Ride to Glendalough—Other Tourists—The Seven Churches—" The Meeting of the Waters "—Avoca.

MOUNTAINS AND LAKES—OLD CASTLES AND TOWNS.	67

An Irish Liberal—Arklow—Shelton Abbey—A Norman Castle—Enniscorthy—New Ross—Irishtown—The Steamer *Ida*—Waterford—The

CONTENTS

Top of the Hill—An Old Shanty—Cork—Patrick Street and Bridge—"The Bells of Shandon"—Blarney Castle—The Blarney Stone—A Scotch Lassie— Bantry — Glengariffe— St. Swithin and Rain—On the Road to Killarney—Tunnels— Kenmare— The Black Valley— The Upper Lake.

THE GAP OF DUNLOE—ROMANTIC IRELAND . . . 105

The Royal Victoria Hotel—Ross Castle—To the Gap of Dunloe—Kate Kearney's Cottage—Fairy Glen—Serpent Lake—St. Patrick's Cottage—Macgillicuddy's Reeks—Five Islands—The Long Range—"The Happy Family"—Shooting the Rapids—The Old Bridge—"Toothache Bridge"—Brickeen Bridge—Devil's Island—Muckross Abbey—Colleen Bawn Rock—Torc Mountain — Limerick — The Theatre Royal—The River Shannon—Kilrush.

KILKEE — GALWAY —CLIFDEN —SLIGO —BY RAIL AND RIVER 135

Kilkee—The Cliffs—Dunlicky Castle and Bishop's Island— "Evicted Houses"—The Main Street —Caves of Kilkee— Keeping the Sabbath— Galway— Eyre Square—Church of St. Nicholas— Salmon Leap—Fish Market—Salt Hill—On the Road to Clifden—The New Railroad— Rainbow— Clifden— The Way to Westport—Letterfrack—Kylemore Castle—Leenane—Westport—Ride to Sligo—Rapids—Ballysodare—Sligo—Lough Hill—Our Old Driver—

CONTENTS

The White Donkey — Stories by the Way — Drumcliffe Round Tower — Cliffs on the Glencar — Going for Turf — Bundoran.

FAMOUS IRISH TOWNS AND THEIR INDUSTRIES — THE GIANT'S CAUSEWAY 175
Bundoran — Along the Cliffs — Ballyshannon — Falls of Erne — Belleek Pottery — Lough Erne — Crevinish Castle — Devenish Abbey and Round Tower — Enniskillen — Londonderry — Lough Swilly — The Old Wall — Portrush — Giant's Causeway — Recognizing a Philadelphian — The Organ — Honeycomb — Loom — Lord Antrim's Parlor — The Fan — Keystone — Ladies' Wishing Chair — Old Women — The Chimneys — The Well — The Giant's Eyeglass — Dunluce Castle — Belfast — The Wanamaker of Belfast — Royal Damask Linen Factory — Ormeau Park — Cave Hill — Irish Hospitality.

THE LAND OF BURNS — GLASGOW — THE TROSSACHS. 209
Larne — Stranraer — The Land of Burns — Ayr — Burns' Cottage — The Monument — Relics of the Poet — Picture — Glasgow — Origin of the Name — Royal Princess Theatre — About the City — The Cathedral — West End Park — James Watt — The Clyde — Loch Lomond — The Trossachs — Inversnaid — Loch Katrine — Rob Roy's Hut — Stronachlachar — Ellen's Isle — Our Coach — Loch Ard.

THE HIGHLANDS — STAFFA AND IONA — FINGAL'S CAVE — INVERNESS 233
Greenock — *En Route* for Oban — Dunoon — Rothesay — Kyles of Bute — Maids of Bute —

CONTENTS

Tarbert—Crinan Canal—Oban—Castle Dunstaffnage—Staffa—Fingal's Cave—The Causeway—Bending Pillars—Fingal's Wishing Chair—Iona—The Street of the Dead—The Cemetery—Ballachulish—Glencoe—Ossian's Cave—The Scene of the Massacre—Banavie—Ben Nevis—Fort Augustus—Inverness—The Northern Meeting—Scotch Pipers—A Noted Character—Away to Edinburgh—Scenes on the Journey—Farewell to the Highlands.

EDINBURGH AND THE ENGLISH LAKES—THE HOME VOYAGE 281

Edinburgh — The Castle — Princes Street—Scott's Monument—St. Giles' Cathedral—Canongate Tolbooth — John Knox's House and Church — White Horse Close — Holyrood — Queen Mary's Apartments—The Queensferry Road—Dean Bridge—Forth Bridge—Farewell to Scotland—Keswick—Lake Derwentwater—Pencil Manufacturers—Greta Hall—The Islands—Drive Around the Lake—By Coach to Windermere—Homes of Shelley and Hall Caine—Wythburn Church — Lake Thirlmere — Helm Crag—Grasmere—Nab Cottage—Rydal Mount Ambleside—Windermere—Liverpool—The Day of Departure — On Board the *Etruria*— The Home Voyage—New York—Home Again.

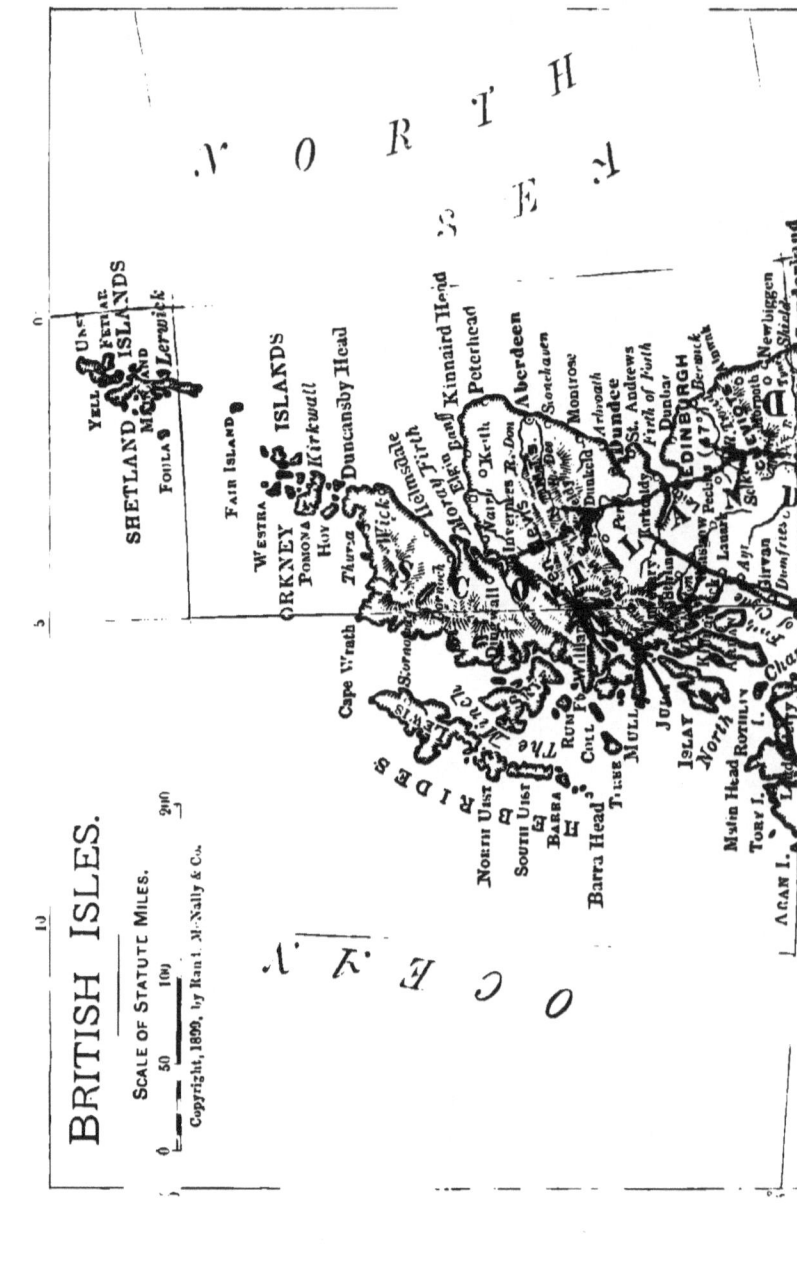

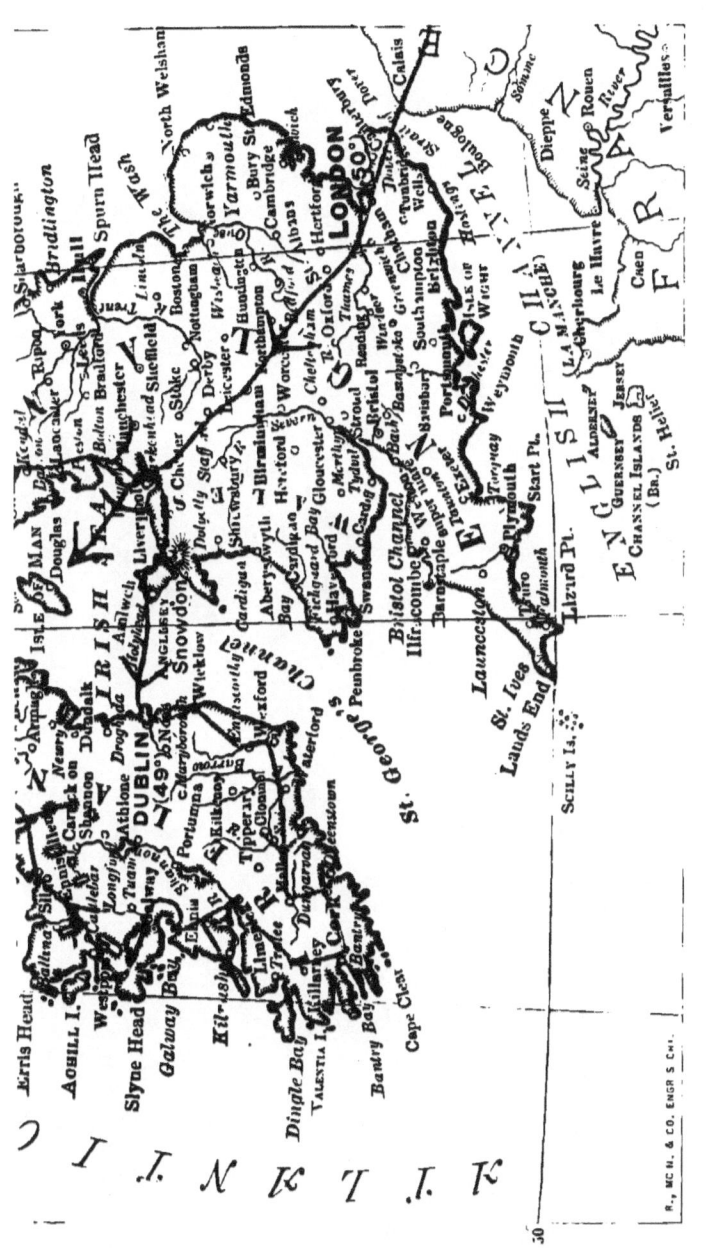

LIST OF ILLUSTRATIONS

	PAGE
"Here are many pigs, the 'Gentlemen who pay the rent'"	*Frontispiece*
"The Irish Jaunting Car"	41
Bray, the Brighton of Ireland	47
The Famous Glendalough	57
Sweet Vale of Avoca	63
"Irishtown"	71
"As we ascend, we pass through the very old part of Waterford"	77
"Dried-up specimens of humanity"	81
"Blarney Castle was a lordly place in the days of its glory"	85
"We leave with reluctance this delightful spot"	89
"We pass through a tunnel"	93
"A magnificent view meets our eyes"	97
"Royal Victoria Hotel, Killarney"	101
"Old Ross Castle, Killarney"	109
Fairy Glen and Serpent Lake, Gap of Dunloe	113
"The musicians, however, are anything but fairy-like"	117
"We shoot the Rapids under Old Weir Bridge"	121
Devil's Island, Killarney	125
Colleen Bawn Rock	129
"In the Distance is Bishop's Island"	139
Main Road, Galway	143
"We have never seen their like before"	147
"We find ourselves within sight of the beautiful and picturesque Kylemore Castle"	151
"We take our places in the large jaunting car that leaves for Sligo"	155

LIST OF ILLUSTRATIONS

	PAGE
"Picturesque mountains are on our right"	159
"We have an old driver full of Irish wit and history"	163
"We pass many children on donkeys with baskets on either side, going for turf"	167
"There are many odd sights"	171
Great Northern Hotel, Bundoran	179
"How skilful these workmen are in moulding the many different patterns"	183
"Exquisite scenes greet us on right and left"	187
"Port Coon Cave"	191
"View of the Famous Causeway"	195
"Surrounding the chair are many old women"	199
"The little cottage in which Burns was born"	215
"Enchanting scenery surrounds us," Loch Lomond	225
"We are rowed to the Island"	241
"The renowned Fingal's Cave"	245
"We walk along the 'Street of the Dead'"	251
"We have reached the scene of the massacre"	257
"We have a fine view of Ben Nevis"	261
"We have a long and delightful ride on Loch Ness"	265
"A Prize Dance"	269
"A Typical Highland Washday"	274
"Queen's View, Killiecrankie Pass"	277
"The famous bridge which spans the Forth"	295
"We Stroll to Lake Derwentwater"	301
"The Quiet Waters of Rydal"	311

Abroad—Paris—

" Merrie England."

Abroad—Paris—"Merrie England."

Sail for Havre—Paris—Champs Elysées—Bois de Boulogne—St. Cloud—The Louvre—Tuileries—Place de la Concorde—Versailles—Père la Chaise—London—Clean Streets — The Tower of London — British Museum—Westminster Abbey—Hampton Court—St. Paul's Cathedral—Crystal Palace—Planning a Tour—Ireland, Scotland, and the English Lakes—London Street Cries—Living Expenses at Home and Abroad — We Leave London — Travelling Companions—Liverpool—A Bank Holiday—New Brighton—Salvationists—Parliament.

MANY human beings deem it one of Heaven's greatest blessings to be "let alone;" to be allowed to wander on, day after day, along the beaten track of familiar routine; to pass their whole lives amid the associations of their native cities: while others desire more than the comforts of a home surrounded by dear friends and relatives, and long for a personal knowledge of distant countries, and the manners and customs of their inhabitants.

In the hearts of the latter class, the years as they come and go, leave germs of restlessness, and a gradually increasing determination to gratify this longing; to add to their experience by a visit to these foreign shores; to tramp and observe the rare, the new, the curious; to see life in all its phases; and to fill the mental storehouse with the varied treasures that only thus may be obtained. This is the case with us. And so we find ourselves one day on board the French Liner *La Bourgogne*, bound for Havre, in order to make a roundabout trip, and take in Paris, on our way to the British Isles.

As the great hawsers which hold the steamer to the pier are loosened, and we are towed toward midstream, we strain our eyes to distinguish the forms of the dear ones assembled on the end of the pier to wish us *bon voyage*. Other emotions mingle with the joy of starting out to fulfil our dreams, and observe the possibilities in life on other planes. The good wishes and loving calls of farewell lose their sweetness in the noise and bustle that prevail, and our only consolation is in the continued waving of handkerchiefs. These little white signals speak to us in place of the lips that are sealed, and we watch them fondly until the increasing distance shuts them wholly from view ; then seek steamer chairs, and write letters to the dear ones, to be taken ashore by the pilot, when he leaves us at Sandy Hook.

So the first day passes in writing and lounging on deck, enjoying the pure sea air. What follows during the ensuing days until we reach Havre need hardly be noted. It is the same from day to day ; the noise of the machinery, the roll of the steamer, encouraging words to the sick, and the usual round of entertainments found on an ocean steamer : so the time passes, while our staunch ship ploughs the angry waves, or glides smoothly over the waters of the deep blue sea. We reach Havre at eleven o'clock in the evening, and remain on board till morning. Many pleasant acquaintances have been made during the voyage, and now regretful partings, accompanied by "May Heaven bless you" and hopes of future meetings are the order of the day. We proceed by train from Havre to Paris the same day, and drive to the Normandy Hotel.

We remain a couple of weeks in the gay capital. Many and varied are the pleasures afforded by this wonderful city. In our expeditions about the city we frequently come across a fellow voyager, an acquaintance, or an old friend from home; and these unexpected meetings are a source of great delight to us, since we are never sure that an entertaining companion will not fall in with us at any point in our merry journeys hither and thither. The streets are full of life and the Champs Elysées, as ever, stands without a rival, as the centre of gayety and beauty. This charming place is frequented by all classes of the people. There are many seats in the shade of its fine trees, and for a penny, you may occupy one for an hour or a day, according to your pleasure. Thousands of maidens and pretty children may be seen flitting about these lovely walks. Numerous cafés offer refreshments to the pleasure seekers, and there are concert halls, with their mimic stages for dancers and actors, while the lover of music, from him who prefers the typical French songs of the day to the worshipper of more classic melodies, will here find his taste gratified. We pay our penny, and from an enchanting bower look out upon the happy throng during a long delightful afternoon. In the Bois de Boulogne we also find the merry populace, driving along in fashionable attire, strolling through the Park, or lingering beside the lake and waterfall. The fine avenue from the Champs Elysées hither is a pleasant sight in afternoons, when the throng of gay equipages is at its height.

The village of St. Cloud is several miles west of Paris, on the Seine; and here are the famous palace, gardens and park. The palace is a ruin, but the gardens are very lovely, and we wander among the beautiful paths, admiring the world-renowned fountains, and from the tops of the hills which the gardens cover, we have a magnificent view of the city of Paris.

The glorious paintings and wonderful statuary of the Louvre are irresistible attractions, and we spend many hours in the presence of these masterpieces of great artists.

The Garden of the Tuileries is another favorite resort of the people, to whom it is open from daybreak until dark. From its terraces there is a beautiful prospect of the Seine, the Place de la Concorde and the Champs Elysées. The palace, which has been the scene of various historical events and terrible tragedy, is a ruin, inaccessible to the public.

The Place de la Concorde, with its fine views its charming fountains, and its historical associations, also attracts us, and we can scarcely realize that on this beautiful, peaceful spot the infuriated mobs of Paris wrought their deeds of vengeance, and put to death a long line of noble men and women. So lovely are our surroundings here, that that dreadful epoch seems the creation of a morbid fancy, or a terrible nightmare, which we are glad to cast into the shades of oblivion.

But endless are the entertainments, and numberless the interesting and attractive points for the stranger in Paris. It would be vain to attempt to mention them all. Yet I cannot pass by the palace, gardens, and fountains of Versailles without a word. How long could we not linger on those wide terraces, and in those lovely embowered paths, with the shining sheets of water at their feet. We are loath to leave these enchanting vistas, with their fairy-like associations, even for the palace itself. The statuary, bronzes, and vases on the outside are worthy a longer observation than our time will allow, and to do justice to this richly ornamented interior, with its painting and sculpture, with our limited time, would be a vain attempt. We would indeed gladly spend many days in this lovely spot, but Paris and her environments call for a long sojourn or many visits.

In Père la Chaise we find the celebrated tomb of Abelard and Héloise, with its effigies of the lovers lying at last side by side in their long sleep.

But the last days arrive, and we hasten through the remainder of our sight-seeing, bid farewell to the pleasure-loving throngs, and, crossing the English Channel with an indescribable feeling of "homeness" and kinship, find ourselves once more among people who speak our own language.

At Morley's Hotel, Trafalgar Square, London, in response to a telegram, a fine large room is ready for us, with windows overlooking the Strand.

London is a beautiful city. Each time we visit this metropolis we are more impressed with the order and cleanliness of its streets. We are informed that they are flushed with water every morning at about three o'clock. There are hosts of boys whose duty it is to gather up all the litter that may be seen defacing the highways.

We do not remain at Morley's, but settle

down in apartments in a very comfortable house in Duchess Street, Portland Place, where we have a large chamber and a spacious, elaborately furnished drawing-room or library. We are located in one of the most desirable spots in London, convenient to theatres, shops, etc. Our stay here is pleasant and full of interest. We travel about in the most unconventional manner, stopping wherever the impulse of the moment leads us. Some days the beautiful Thames tempts us with its famous and picturesque bridges and the noble country-seats along its banks. We wander out to Richmond Hill for the lovely view, or linger about Hyde Park in the late afternoon to see the carriages and equestrians on "Rotten Row." In the South Kensington Museum we prowl about in the most unsystematic manner, now filled with enthusiasm for an ancient Indian god, now absorbed in a rare volume in the magnificent library here, or lost in admiration of a fine English water-color. We spend hours here when the mood for antiquity is upon us.

It is very interesting to watch the mass of people, and the endless rows of vehicles constantly moving over London Bridge. The police are busy keeping everything and everybody moving in the two ceaseless streams, one flowing to the north, the other to the south.

The ancient Tower of London stands on the banks of the Thames, in the heart of the city, and, although built by William the Conqueror, is in a perfect state of preservation. Here we see the long row of king's effigies, from Edward I. to James II., also the crown jewels, and many trophies of war and stands of ancient armor. The treasures of the British Museum are priceless and beyond description. We linger among the Elgin marbles and the other mutilated statuary, whose grace and nobility of form are the dream and the despair of the artists of to-day.

For more than eight hundred years the kings and queens of England have been crowned in Westminster Abbey. Here, too, are royal tombs, and tombs of those who were greater than royalty. Here are monuments and memorials of all the English celebrities of many ages. Here lie the mortal remains of Spenser, Milton, Dryden, of Handel, of Dickens and Thackeray, and many, many others.

Here, too, fastened beneath the celebrated Coronation Chair, is the famous Stone of Scone, with its wonderful history and curious traditions. This dark, rough-looking stone is about two feet square and six or seven inches thick. It is said to be the stone upon which Jacob's head rested when he beheld the vision of the heavenly staircase and the " angels of God." Edward I. brought this stone from Scotland, where for many generations it was the coronation stone of the Scottish kings.

In the National Gallery we see a fine collection of paintings by the great English masters.

The splendid palace of Hampton Court is on the Thames, a short distance from London. The park and gardens are lovely, and the enormous chestnut trees have a world-wide fame. In the palace is a fine gallery of paintings, mostly historical portraits, and there are luxurious apartments and handsome tapestry. The terrace, nearly a mile in length, overlooks a charming landscape.

St. Paul's Cathedral is on the summit of Ludgate Hill, and may be seen from many miles around. It is of gigantic proportions and contains the tombs of many of England's great men.

Kew Garden is the most famous garden in the world. Its trees, bushes, shrubs, and flowers are arranged for artistic effect, and one might explore it for days without ceasing to find new plants or trees or flowers, or unexpected arrangements in its paths or shrubbery.

Meanwhile the all-important question of plans for future travel presents itself. What course shall we pursue next? How and whither shall we go in order to observe the most curious, interesting, and instructive phases of life in this richly-dowered region?

Abroad—Paris—"Merrie England"

The genial and untiring manager at the main office of Thos. Cook & Son is of great assistance in our consultations. He plans for us a route which will include many of the most interesting places for the lovers of old abbeys and picturesque scenery to be found in these localities. By the plan proposed we proceed from London to Liverpool, thence to Dublin and Cork, and by steamer, rail, and coach, skirt the western shore of Ireland, from south to north, until we reach Belfast. There the Scotch map is taken up, with the journey to Glasgow, and delightful winding tours thereabout, to Oban. Thence to the Hebrides; back to Oban again, and along the Caledonian Canal to Inverness, Forres and Edinburgh. Thence to the English Lakes and Liverpool. Many points not mentioned are embraced in this first outline of our prospective tour.

The plan suits us, and tickets are purchased for the entire route. Now follows much reading up of the points of interest to be seen in our travels. We also look so far ahead as to engage a state-room for the return voyage to America on the good steamer *Etruria.*

As I sit reading this morning by the library window, overlooking the street, strange and unintelligible sounds come to my ears from the various venders, who thus advertise their wares.

"Heat! Heat!" cries the man who has coal for sale. The indistinguishable cry of the strawberry man leaves upon the mind the impression of "Strawberry! Strawberry! Very heavy." The milkman calls "Coo! Coo!" and the chimney sweep wails "Screep! Screep! Screep!"

"Qui vive! Qui vive!" is the next sound that greets my ear. What on earth has this man to sell? Looking out the window, I perceive a vender with a large basket. My first inclination is to close the window and return to my book, but no; my curiosity is aroused to such a pitch as the strange cry continues, that I hasten out into the street and follow the fellow, determined to learn what he has in his basket. It proves to be cat and dog meat, which he calls out in such a manner that it sounds exactly like " Qui vive."

These are some of the week-day sounds. On the Sabbath there is a change. The noble church bells with their musical chimes call all good Christians to the House of God to offer thanks to the Ruler of all, for the blessings he has bestowed. Now I hear in the distance the notes of a hymn sung with much pathos. The voices draw nearer and nearer, until beneath our window appear a man, woman, and child, singing as they walk along, and now and then turning aside to solicit alms from their listeners, glad of any mite thrown to them.

We find living abroad quite as expensive as at home; that is, in accordance with our usual mode of living. Vegetables, meats, fruits, etc., average about the same here in price; also entertainments, as theatres, operas, and the like. Clothing seems to be the single exception, and here the cost is from forty to fifty per cent. less. For instance: strawberries, while at their height, cost at a regular fruit store, eighteen and twenty cents a box; cherries, ten, twelve, and sixteen cents a pound; tomatoes, three, four, and five cents apiece. These prices could, however, be reduced by purchasing at one of the many markets for the sale of such produce.

Omnibus fares are to some extent cheaper. The system is more just than ours. Suppose the route to be four miles: the first mile, a fare of one penny is charged; for two miles, the fare is two pennies; for three miles, three pennies, and so on, so that the passenger who travels only one mile is not obliged to pay the fare for the whole route.

Hansom rates are also less than in the United States. For two persons a shilling is charged for one mile, one and sixpence for two miles, and so on. It would seem at this rate as though the fare might become so much reduced that if a "cabby" carries you four miles you pay him nothing, and if six miles the obligation is on the other side, and you receive a premium of a shilling for favor conferred; but thus far my experience has not proved that the analogy has been practically carried out.

As the time for leaving London approaches, the bustle and confusion of packing fill the atmosphere.

We leave the Midland R. R. Station at noon, and by previous arrangement (the payment of a shilling to the guard) are given a first-class compartment in the express train. A little " oil " thus used, causes the machinery of travel to run smoothly.

We suppose we are to be alone, but just before leaving the station learn that another passenger is to share the compartment. Our fellow-traveller is a grave-looking man of about sixty-five years. He at once begins conversation, and after some remarks on religion, politics and general topics of the day, inquires our destination. Upon learning that we are making a tour through Ireland and Scotland, he becomes much interested, and changing his seat for one nearer to us, bids us make notes of the various hotels in both these countries where he is known to the proprietors. We make the notes—partly to satisfy the old man.

He leaves us at Bedford, saying that he feels in better spirits than before he met us. The poor man had lost his wife two years ago, and was in consequence much depressed. He informed us that he was born at Bedford, and had many a time, when a boy, played top near the church where John Bunyan tolled the bell, and swore while doing it.

While we are congratulating ourselves upon being once more alone, the train stops at Leicester, and a lady and gentleman enter our compartment—a tall, handsome type of the Irish gentleman, with a typical English woman for his wife.

The appearance of my camera, arranged to take some photographs of Leicester, opens an interesting conversation between the lady and myself, while her husband engages my companion in an animated talk on hunting, fishing, etc. They are a delightful couple, and we soon become as social as old acquaintances. They are owners of large estates in Ireland, but are too poor to live upon them. They are " land poor." At Derby they leave us with the customary " God bless you " and hearty thanks for our invitation to visit us in America.

We are fortunate enough to have another agreeable fellow-traveller in a young man, with whom we soon find ourselves in animated conversation. He points out all the interesting places along the way, and gives us much valuable information regarding them.

The scenery is grand as we approach the famous Derbyshire Hills. One could more easily imagine himself in some Alpine village than in the heart of England. Here is a tunnel two miles in length, and we are just two minutes and a half passing through it. While in the tunnel, the windows of the car seem to be covered with frost. Our new acquaintance tells us that this is from the action of sulphur, which we smell quite plainly. As we emerge into the daylight our eyes rest upon the beautiful Matlock, which, with the surrounding country, is a paradise of enchanting loveliness.

We pass the Peak Forest, the scene of Sir Walter Scott's famous novel, "Peveril of the Peak," also Buxton and Stockport, large manufacturing centres for cotton goods, and come to the great Manchester Canal, upon which so many millions of dollars have been expended, and which thus far has proved a financial failure. And now at last we whirl into the station at Liverpool, an hour behind schedule time. We have been six hours on the road, and are truly sorry that this portion of our journey has come to an end, so interesting have our fellow-travellers made the way.

Our train is a long one, drawn by two immense engines, and is crowded with passengers, as it is a bank holiday. All stores and business places here are closed to the public, and the entire day is devoted to frolic and pleasure. We go at once to the pleasant and homelike Adelphi Hotel.

Liverpool contains many fine buildings, among them a number of old churches and a handsome art gallery. It also has some pretty parks, with picturesque sheets of water winding among their hills; and there are many quaint old inns on the outskirts of the town, as well as numerous substantial residences surrounded by grand old trees. Everywhere are evidences of the great wealth and vast trade of the city, yet there are too many evidences of poverty and vice.

I avail myself of the present opportunity to make a trip to New Brighton, the sea-shore resort of the people of Liverpool. Here are crowds of men, women, and children bent on pleasure. The enormous passenger traffic on this road is almost beyond calculation, and the sight is a pleasure to those who enjoy large gatherings. New Brighton is situated on the bank of the Mersey, and here, if his bones are not too stiff, one may enjoy bathing, dancing, playing ball, and riding horses and donkeys. He may refresh himself after these exercises with a cup of the celebrated English tea.

This evening we take a "bus" ride and see swarms of people returning home after the day's frolic, all merry and orderly, though tired. Here is an extract from one of the daily newspapers of Liverpool on the subject of bank holidays:

"The weather yesterday may be compared to a man who is excused because his bark is worse than his bite. It threatened a good deal but did little. In the morning it was cold, as it often is in these latitudes. About midday the sun condescended now and again to favor the holiday-makers with a brief and fleeting smile, but the brightness soon vanished, and finally in the evening it rained a little bit, and so we had some of the proverbial 'samples of weather' which seems to be the modern paraphrase for the time-honored 'six fine days and a thunderstorm,' that, as Continental folk are firmly persuaded, is the English summer. Still the British public that goes a-pleasuring on bank holidays is in no wise put out by mild deterrents like these. Such samples of the British public as patronize Liverpool on these occasions—and they come from as near as Wigan, and as far as Newcastle-upon-Tyne, flocking in from all the four quarters of the Midlands and Yorkshire and Lancashire—appear to be well satisfied with things. Well-behaved and orderly crowds, too, they are, and well dressed. The passion for steamboat voyaging, even if only across the Mersey and back, is strong within those whose opportunities of indulging in the pastime are limited. The bank holiday makers appear to find Liverpool interesting enough, in spite of the fact that none of the town people remain in the city who can get away. It is not unpicturesque, its public buildings and its Art Gallery and Museum are worth looking at, and then there is the river, a marine panorama of no mean order, with, on the other side of it, the wild and exhilarating frolics of New Brighton."

Another is as follows: " From an early hour,

trippers poured into New Brighton and the large stretch of sand to the north and south of the promenade pier soon became covered with a moving mass of people. As usual, the arrangements made for the ferry traffic were excellent, the whole of the fleet of the Wallasey Local Board, some nine steamers, being in requisition."

Liverpool seems to be a centre for the "Salvationists," for at almost every corner one sees a great crowd of people uniting in religious services and singing hymns, the leader having a portable organ or accordion. At one corner the minister is entreating his hearers to come into the church, which is about to open its doors close by, and many probably follow his advice, as there seems to be an inclination towards religion here, in spite of much wickedness and uncleanliness.

We attend the Royal Alexandra Theatre, which proves but a second-rate entertainment. In purchasing reserved seats at places of amusement throughout England it is customary to register the name of the buyer in the regular books as well as inscribe it upon his slip.

To-morrow we will be again *en route*, by train and steamer, for Dublin *via* Holyhead, hoping to reach our destination by half-past five in the afternoon.

There has been an exciting election for members of Parliament in England. While these elections are affairs of great importance, and arouse public feeling to a considerable degree, they do not in any respect resemble the scenes at some of our polls, such, for instance, as the disgraceful riots carried on during election day in the Fourth Ward in Philadelphia, which have frequently been anything but a credit to the reputation of a well-governed city. It is quite common in England for the ladies to take an active part in the elections, soliciting votes for their favorite candidates, and in many ways exerting a widespread and powerful influence in public affairs. Indeed, a prominent English lady assured me that she had secured a large number of votes for a member recently elected.

Dublin, Bray, and

Picturesque Ireland.

Dublin, Bray, and Picturesque Ireland.

En route for Dublin—Holyhead—Kingstown—Dublin—An Irish Jaunting Car—Petticoat Lane—Sackville Street—Hill of Howth—Bray—Enniskerry—Glen of the Downs—Esplanade—A Little Irish Boy—Sketching Bray Head—Spectators—Sugar Loaf Mountain—Rathdrum—The Ride to Glendalough—Other Tourists—The Seven Churches—"The Meeting of the Waters"—Avoca.

WE leave the station of the L. & N. W. R.W., Liverpool, for Dublin, at 10.25 a. m., with two steamer trunks and our hand-grips. It is a charming day. Heavy clouds hang in the sky, illuminated by the radiant sunbeams with picturesque effect. We pass through the northern part of Wales, and from Rhyl onward behold a scenic panorama of great grandeur. On our right is the long expanse of the Irish Sea, while on the left the beautiful mountains of Wales tower far above us.

There are many watering-places along the

route, with their unsightly bathing machines stationed here and there on the edge of the beach. As we speed on, making a mile a minute, we leave behind us Rhyl, Colwin, Bangor, and at last arrive at Holyhead, where we take a fine, powerful steamer, the *Connaught*, for Kingstown. There is a great hurrying hither and thither of men, women, and children, with boxes, satchels, and bundles. The whistle sounds, the great side wheels begin to turn, the water foams and bubbles, and we are under full steam for old Ireland.

It is a charming voyage. The steamer makes good time, and, sitting on deck, we watch the lofty mountains of Wales soften into hills, then banks, and finally disappear wholly from our view, while the tall peaks of Ireland rise up to claim their share of the universal enthusiasm. The great hill of Howth—and Howth itself—now appear in full view. We pass the Kisk Light-ship, and, looking south, behold Kingstown, the port for which we are destined.

"The Irish Jaunting Car"

Now ensues a general stampede, and in the bustle and confusion of landing every one seems in terror lest "the devil catch the hindmost." All, however, reach the shore in safety, and a train bears us from Kingstown to Dublin in a few minutes. Here we soon find ourselves in comfortable quarters in the Hotel Metropole, on Sackville Street.

In a short walk about the city after dinner we have a glimpse of some of Dublin's lads and lasses, and are highly entertained by our first sight of the Irish jaunting car, which is here used both as a private equipage and a hired vehicle. It will be an interesting experiment to learn how one can ride sideways, with his feet dangling over the wheels of the car. We will try it to-morrow.

We are up bright and early and engage our jaunting car at one and sixpence an hour for a ride around the city. It must be confessed this is rather an odd affair to the uninitiated. Unless one holds on with a firm grip, he stands a good chance of being thrown from his seat on suddenly turning a corner. We drive for an hour through the principal streets, passing many handsome hotels, residences, shops, and other interesting buildings. Sackville Street is the chief thoroughfare, and we find it most attractive, while Grafton Street, the shopping and business locality, presents a mass of stores, especially pleasing to the visitor who comes hither with a well-filled pocket-book.

Our drive includes the Bank of Ireland, a noble-looking building, with an imposing colonnade, once the meeting-place of the Irish Parliament, and filled with historical associations. We also pass Trinity College, with its spacious buildings of Portland stone, six hundred feet in depth. It is of the Corinthian order. In the background is a beautiful park, adorned with fine trees and of considerable extent, which is used exclusively by the students.

The Castle of Dublin, at the west end of Dame Street, is situated in spacious grounds, but is by no means imposing in appearance, and has little to distinguish it from other ancient buildings. Close by is Christ Church Cathedral, which dates back to 1038, and is noted as the repository for various relics : it contains, among others, the monumental tomb of Strongbow, Earl of Pembroke, the invader of Ireland.

Here is the Cathedral of St. Patrick, the original building of which, it is said, was erected by St. Patrick himself, near the well in which he baptized his converts. Nelson's Monument, a tall column, stands beside the Post Office, which is a very handsome building of granite, with a fine portico, supported by fluted columns, and surmounted by noble statuary.

The Four-Courts is a magnificent structure, facing the river Liffey, with a front 450 feet in length.

Phœnix Park, the delight of the people of Dublin, is a grand old place, covering more than seventeen hundred acres of ground. It is a lovely picturesque region, with nature's own effects preserved in the beautiful green grass, ancient trees and luxuriant shrubbery, with long vistas, disclosing charming views of the Wicklow Mountains. It is said to be the largest park in Britain.

Many other interesting spots greet our eyes as we drive about Dublin. Few cities of its size can boast of a greater number of handsome and useful buildings. But they do not comprise the whole of the town, as we learn, when, by way of contrast, we turn into "Petticoat Lane," as it is termed. It would be difficult to imagine anything more utterly forlorn than this street, with its mingling of filth and rags. Water appears to be utterly unknown here. Men, women and children crowd around the saleswomen, who shout at the top of their voices, urging the populace to buy their wares — disreputable-looking articles of every description: shoes, old and torn; worn and filthy garments that would disgrace a refuse heap. These are offered at prices to suit the class of purchasers. The sight is beyond description, and we are satisfied with a brief survey of this portion of the town.

BRAY, THE BRIGHTON OF IRELAND

Here is the Drogheda Railway Station, and we are starting on an excursion to the peninsula, known as the Hill of Howth, nine miles north of Dublin. The ride is delightful, for majestic mountains loom up in the distance on either side. The threatened rain has become a reality before we arrive at Howth; however, we are not discouraged, but engaging a jaunting car we ascend the Hill. Here we bid our driver go his way, that we may enjoy the magnificent view undisturbed.

The Hill of Howth is the most admired of all the beautiful suburbs of Dublin. It is six hundred feet high, jutting out into the sea, and guarding the entrance to the river. It commands a glorious view, and descends steeply to the water which dashes against its base. The Liffey flows upon one side of its cliffs, while a deep bay or harbor is on the other.

We stroll about in the rain for a couple of hours, enjoying the extensive prospect around us. Toward the north we can see a curious rocky island, which is known as Ireland's Eye, and beyond this, Lambey, equally charming, with a different kind of beauty. Howth Castle, not far from the railway station, is surrounded by extensive grounds, well laid out, and the Abbey is in the village, overlooking the harbor.

To-day we proceed to Bray, a fashionable watering-place, sometimes styled "The Brighton of Ireland," about twelve miles south of Dublin. It has a population of perhaps seven thousand. We take rooms at the Royal Marine Hotel, which faces the sea, and after lunching, make a tour of the place in a jaunting car.

As far as the eye can see, mountains upon mountains rise, from twelve hundred to fifteen hundred feet above the level of the sea, presenting beautiful and varied views on every side. Before us is a picturesque settlement of small one-story houses, with whitewashed walls and thatched roofs.

As we ride through Enniskerry, we see in the distance the great Sugar Loaf Mountain, which is sixteen hundred and eighty-one feet above the sea.

The road to the Glen of the Downs is smooth and delightful. Here we meet many ladies and gentlemen on bicycles. They walk up, and coast down these hilly highways. The Glen is about a mile and a half long, and runs along the foot of the Downs Mountain. Its sides, which rise to a height of six hundred feet, are densely covered with copsewood.

There are many private demesnes in and around Bray, to which the public are admitted only on certain days of the week. We drive to one of these, the estate of the Earl of Meath, which encompasses Sugar Loaf Mountain, but the gate to the entrance is locked, also that to Bray Head; and in spite of all our persuasions, they remain locked. The keeper is not to be bribed—evidently shillings are plentiful in his experience—so we give it up.

The Esplanade, or Promenade, is of solid stone masonry. Here we stroll frequently, meeting the fashionable population of Bray, and observing the few who venture to take a dip in the ocean. Bray Head looms up before us, picturesque and attractive. A path leads around it, commanding many beautiful views, and the enormous tunnel, cut through it by the railway company, is plainly visible from this point.

As we walk along we see before us a fat little Irish boy, round and smiling, with such bright blue eyes that I must capture him, if not by camera, by pencil. He turns to admire the sea, all unconscious, and I make a rapid sketch of him in my note book.

> An Irish youngster, with form so round,
> Cheeks so red, and eyes so blue—
> Legs bowed, dress loose, and every pound
> Just fat—he stands a type so true.

Looking north we see Killiney Hill jutting far out into the bay. The view from this hill is one of the loveliest in this region. Beside the bay with its stately ships, one looks down on Kingstown and across to the old Hill of Howth.

This afternoon I settle myself in the most favorable spot for making a water-color sketch of Bray Head, and in a position, as I suppose, free from all observers. It is at the foot of a stone wall, and I am getting on nicely with my picture and congratulating myself on the "attend-to-your-own-business" air of the people around, when, happening to glance toward the promenade overhead, I become aware of a dozen or more interested spectators. I cannot tell whether this interest is complimentary or otherwise. However, I go on with my work, and they stay until the sketch is finished.

We leave Bray this morning for Rathdrum. On the way we pass through several tunnels in Bray Head. Sugar Loaf Mountain is visible from the car window. How noble and majestic it looks. It seems to send down a benediction as we bid farewell to the beautiful picture.

The day is fine, and everything favors our journey. On the train we make the acquaintance of a pleasant and hospitable Irish gentleman, who not only gives us much information regarding his native country, but invites us to spend a day or two at his castle at Enniscorthy. We thank him, but decline the sincere invitation.

At Rathdrum about twenty jaunting cars await the tourists who wish to visit famous Glendalough and the Seven Churches. Leaving our luggage at the Railroad Hotel, we select a car to our liking—that is, one in which there is plenty of room. There are six other tourists in our car, all making the trip to Glendalough, and at least twelve of the remaining cars are filled with passengers for the same destination.

The day begins favorably, but in a half hour the rain pours down upon us. We are, fortunately, well protected by waterproofs and umbrellas, having had previous experiences of the uncertainty of Irish weather. Our road lies through a most gorgeous and beautiful country, and, although the rain deprives us of the more extended views, we enjoy the mountains that rise far above us on every side and the picturesque valley below. Our travelling companions are lively and agreeable. An Englishman and his sister, as well as the three gentlemen who sit opposite, prove most entertaining. You will perhaps wonder at this statement when I add that the latter are deaf and dumb; also that we do not seem to realize their inability to hear and speak. There are in their party twenty or thirty deaf-mutes, who are attending a congress at Dublin. One of them is from Philadelphia, and is an exceedingly fine man.

In our whole party eight countries are represented—England, Ireland, Scotland, America, Turkey, Armenia, India, and France. We ride on and on, through the beautiful country of Avondale, seeing many lovely bits of scenery. This is the home of Parnell. Many of the people come out of their shanties and cheer us, looking meanwhile for the pennies that are thrown to them in return.

Now we are in the valley, driving along picturesque wooded roads—now on the height of a mountain path with the prospect stretching out miles before us. Here is the vale of Clara; here Derry Bawn. The succession of charming views which delight the eyes seems endless. Indeed there is no portion of this region that is without interest.

At last we are within sight of famous Glendalough, whose singular beauty and celebrated ruins are the subjects of many legends and traditions. There are seven ruins of ancient churches in this region. I can do no better than to copy here some extracts from the guide book, for those who may be interested:

"The founder of Glendalough was Kevin, signifying in Irish the fair born, whose descent on both sides was from the royal stock of Leinster. The date of his birth is unknown; he died in the year 618. Shortly after being ordained a priest, Kevin withdrew to the wilderness of Glendalough, a valley shut in by lofty mountains, and lived here seven years as a hermit. His dwelling on the northern shore of the lake was a hollow

The Famous Glendalough

tree; on the southern shore he lived in a very narrow cave, to which there was no access except by boat, for it is overhung by a perpendicular rock of great height. His retreat was discovered by a shepherd, and crowds flocked to see him. They built him a cell close to the southern shore of the lake, and an oratory hard by. This place soon became too small for the multitude of disciples who sought to dwell around his little church, and, at the bidding of an angel, he erected the monastery of " The Valley of the Two Lakes," which was the parent of many others. St. Saviour's Monastery is on the opposite side of the river. Here are also Kevin's Cross, Kevin's Kitchen, St. Mary's Church, Rhefert's Church, and other ruins."

All these traditional spots are very interesting, and St. Kevin's Bed may be seen at the upper lake. There is a superstition that a wish made here will be fulfilled.

On our return to Rathdrum a change of clothing, supplemented by a glass of " Irish

Mountain Dew," counteracts any tendency to take cold after our wet excursion.

We meet here, as elsewhere, the well-known Irish wit, who has an answer ready for all questions, and who triumphs over his opponent in repartee.

The first thing we do on awakening this Sunday morning is to look out the window for the weather indications. Alas, the rain is coming down in torrents. We must go to Avoca, and the question is, Shall we travel by rail or coach? The road is most attractive. We wait, hoping it will clear. Yes, it does look brighter, and we order a close carriage with two horses. A vehicle appears which, I am sure, has not seen the daylight for a twelve month, and we start for Avoca, a distance of seven or eight miles. We have not gone far when our driver, a bright typical Irishman, stops his horses, jumps out in the rain and comes to the carriage door to tell us that here is the first "Meeting of the Waters" where the Avonbeg and Avonmore Rivers unite and flow down the vale under the name of the Avoca—that this is the spot mentioned by Thomas Moore as the " valley so sweet." We are in the valley of Cronbane, and have the pleasure of being sheltered for five minutes under the noble oak which shaded the poet when he wrote his famous verses :

There is not in the wide world a valley so sweet
As that vale in whose bosom the bright waters meet ;
Oh ! the last rays of feeling and life must depart,
Ere the bloom of that valley shall fade from my heart.

Yet it *was* not that nature had shed o'er the scene
Her purest of crystal and brightest of green ;
'Twas *not* her soft magic of streamlet or hill,
Oh ! no,—it was something more exquisite still.

'Twas that friends, the beloved of my bosom, were near,
Who made each dear scene of enchantment more dear,
And who felt how the best charms of nature improve,
When we see them reflected from looks that we love.

Sweet vale of Avoca ! how calm could I rest
In thy bosom of shade, with the friends I love best,
Where the storms that we feel in this cold world
      should cease,
And our hearts, like thy waters, be mingled in peace.

The railway runs through the Vale of Avondale, following the Avonmore River, which it crosses several times, affording exquisite glimpses of scenery, and passing the old copper and sulphur mines. Standing below the bridge, and looking up and down river and dale, wood and hill, we have a picture of rare beauty at this junction of the Avonmore and Avonbeg. From this point may be seen, airily poised on the mountain top, the beautiful Castle Howard, the seat of Howard Brooks. This enchanting spot is most inspiring. It really seems that if one would yield himself up to the spirit of the place, thoughts would flow in such poetry as that which has already won the plaudits of the world. I do not know, however, what effect the present deluge might have upon the ardors of a poet.

Moving on to Avoca, we soon reach an attractive hotel, "The Wooden Bridge," where we engage rooms for the day and night. Just below the hotel there is a second "Meeting of the Waters," where the River Aughrim flows into the Avoca.

Sweet Vale of Avoca

We ride about this lovely country for several hours in a jaunting car. To-morrow we will make our way to New Ross, *en route* for Cork.

Before bidding farewell to this beautiful, yes, very beautiful region, we ascend the mountain at the back of the hotel, in company with an agreeable Englishman, also a guest here. On the summit we have a fine view of the Vale, and a magnificent prospect of four mountains, a scene utterly beyond description.

Farewell, sweet Vale of Avoca; thy beauty is far greater than all the words that have been written in thy praise.

Mountains and Lakes—

Old Castles and Towns.

Mountains and Lakes—Old Castles and Towns.

An Irish Liberal—Arklow—Shelton Abbey—A Norman Castle—Enniscorthy—New Ross—Irishtown — The Steamer *Ida*—Waterford—The Top of the Hill—An Old Shanty—Cork—Patrick Street and Bridge—"The Bells of Shandon"—Blarney Castle—The Blarney Stone—A Scotch Lassie—Bantry—Glengariffe—St. Swithin and Rain—On the Road to Killarney—Tunnels—Kenmare—The Black Valley—The Upper Lake.

THE train is fully an hour late, in consequence of an accident at the station above Avoca. While waiting for it we engage in conversation with an old Irish Liberal standing by; a firm believer in the G. O. M. He is a brave old fellow; very staunch and true. When I remark upon his boldness in expressing himself so freely, he replies that England is free in that respect.

Our first station is Arklow, one of the most

important fishing places in Ireland. About a mile and a half farther on is the entrance to the demesne of Shelton, with its beautiful mansion, in the Abbey-Gothic style, surrounded by a fine park. Here, it is said, James II. spent a night during his memorable flight to Waterford, after the battle of the Boyne.

Passing stations Covey and Ferns, with a view of Vinegar Hill in the distance, we approach Enniscorthy. An old Norman castle of fine architectural beauty looms up near us. This is a very pretty country. While not in such a high state of cultivation as the region about Dublin, it possesses a charm that captures the heart of the traveller. Enniscorthy is a thriving town, pleasantly situated on the River Slaney, in the midst of a smiling country. The old Norman castle in its centre was founded, it is said, by Raymond le Gros. In the reign of Elizabeth it was given to the poet Spenser as a residence, and was finally granted to Wallop, the founder of the Portsmouth family, who are lords of the soil.

"IRISHTOWN"

New Ross, seventeen miles from Enniscorthy, is a good town of more than six thousand inhabitants, situated on the River Barrow. Its ancient name is derived from the Irish word Ros, denoting a wooded point overhanging the river.

We arrive here at 4.30 p. m., and proceed to the Royal Hotel.

Although the rain is falling fast, we engage a jaunting car, and clad in waterproofs, go forth to see the town. This is necessary, as we leave early to-morrow, by the steamer *Ida*, for Waterford. Our ride is well worth a ducking, for what we see here will never be forgotten. In New Ross are ancient houses, many of them doubtless several hundred years old, of one story, with stone floors, and in many of them stalls, which seem to have divided the family or families. Ragged and dirty people now inhabit these quarters, which are known as " Irishtown."

With some difficulty I obtain photographs of the most interesting places passed in our drive. This is a grand opportunity for studying old and typical Irish faces. These weather-beaten old men and women are most interesting.

Leaving New Ross we sail down the River Barrow. It is a lovely day. The country along this winding stream is picturesque, although many of the homesteads are in a neglected condition—sad evidence of the poverty of their owners.

In a couple of hours we behold, in the distance, the town of Waterford, and soon find ourselves upon its shore. Now, our first questions are: "When do we leave?" and "How shall we go?"

Our tickets carry us from Waterford to Cappoquin, thence by steamer down the Blackwater River to Youghal, and by rail to Cork: but we learn that the Blackwater is a small stream, and the steamer can make the trip only at high tide. To go by this route we must remain over night at Cappoquin, and take the boat in the morning. This does not suit us at all. Upon inquiry, we ascertain that we can take a train from Waterford this afternoon, change cars at

Fermoy and Mallow, and arrive in Cork this evening. Having decided on this course, we have several hours before us, so we go through the usual programme; that is, take a jaunting car and see the town.

In many of the villages and towns in the South of Ireland, the women wear a shawl thrown over the head, in place of a hat or bonnet. The custom is almost universal in these localities.

Driving along the quay, the first object of interest to us is the ruin of an old tower, called "Reginald's Tower." The name Waterford, or the "Ford of the Father," was bestowed upon the town by the Danes. The place seems to have existed from a very early period, but it did not assume importance until the middle of the ninth century. The town, situated on the Suir, here crossed by a wooden bridge of thirty-nine arches, was anciently known as the "Haven of the Sun," and afterwards as the "Valley of Lamentation," from the tremendous conflicts which took place here between the Irish and the Danes. Reginald's Tower on the Mall, is on the site of the Danish stronghold founded by Reginald, son of Imar. In 1711, when the town was seized by Strongbow and Raymond le Gros, all the Danes were put to death with the exception of the Prince and a few others.

There is a good quay here and an attractive park; also a Protestant church and a handsome Catholic edifice. The old clock is a fine piece of architecture. From its isolated position its face can be seen from a great distance.

Although the quay is many blocks in extent, the principal business portion is confined to the radius of a few squares. There are many old stores, of little interest to the visitor. The people move slowly, and seem to lack utterly our "American rush." From the quay we drive to the top of the hill for a view of the town. As we ascend, we pass through the very old part of Waterford, and see many stone houses of one story, and such ancient dried-up specimens

"AS WE ASCEND, WE PASS THROUGH THE VERY OLD PART OF WATERFORD."

of humanity peering through the windows and standing in the door-ways, that we seem to have come across a generation born at the time of the erection of their houses, several hundred years ago.

We reach Cork safely shortly before nine o'clock in the evening, and go to the Royal Victoria Hotel. This morning we drive about the city; now along the quay, which, at points here and there, shows signs of considerable activity; now through the grounds of Queen's College, which are beautifully laid out, and extend over many acres. The college is an imposing granite structure. Now we are on Patrick Street, the principal shopping street of Cork. Here is Patrick's Bridge, a good substantial piece of architecture.

Along the Sunday Well Road to the top of the hill we go, and have a fine view of the city. There are many beautiful churches in view; the Cathedral of St. Finn Barr is the handsomest of these. There are also numerous large convents, schools, and other institutions in Cork, and, as the population is somewhat less than a hundred thousand, it is astonishing that the place has been enriched with so many fine buildings. But we learn that the institutions are patronized by the adjoining counties, and are well filled at all times.

From the hill-top we see in the distance Cork Harbor, and now St. Vincent's Chapel and School; and now the Church of Shandon, made famous by the poem of the Rev. Francis Mahoney—" The Sweet Bells of Shandon:"

> " With deep affection
> And recollection,
> I often think on
> Those Shandon bells,
> Whose sounds so wild would
> In the days of childhood,
> Fling round my cradle
> Their magic spells.
>
> " I have heard bells chiming
> Full many a clime in,
> Tolling sublime in
> Cathedral shrine;

"Dried Up Specimens of Humanity"

> While at a glib rate
> Brass tongues would vibrate,
> But all their music
> Spoke nought like thine."

We take the tramway to Blarney Castle, which we reach after a pleasant but not especially interesting ride of an hour. A guide with lighted candle leads us through the subterranean passage, where we see many small dungeons—horrible and dismal places, and cruel mementos of that barbarous age when a lifetime spent in those gloomy depths was no uncommon punishment. Blarney Castle was a lordly place in the days of its glory, commanding a fine view over lake and meadow, and the famous Groves of Blarney. Now the walls, from eight to ten feet thick, are a mass of ivy-covered ruins, and happily there are only the landmarks of its places of torture, by which to measure the world's progress in civilization and education.

Of course we see the wonderful Blarney Stone, which is said to impart the gift of eloquence to him who kisses it. The stone hangs at such a dizzy height that it is almost impossible to reach it, but I resort to an expedient, since "All is fair in love and war." Touching the stone with the end of my stick, I kiss that, and now feel gifted with enough Blarney words to bear me through the remainder of this earthly existence.

This evening we attend a play at the Cork Opera House, and are disappointed in the drama, the acting and the actors, as well as in the audience. Everything is second-rate. This is the only opera house or theatre in Cork.

While at Blarney Castle we met a young Scotch lady from Ford Loch Awe, near Loch Gelphead, thirty miles from Oban. She was very entertaining, telling us that Scotland is such a "ferry pretty place," and that we would like her people, whose hospitality to strangers is such, that once their confidence is won, they become true and lasting friends.

We start this morning for Bantry, on our

"Blarney Castle was a lordly place in the days of its glory"

way to Glengariffe. The train makes a long stop at Bandon—long enough for dinner—but when we reach the next station, which is named Desert, we wait hardly a minute, which brings forth many puns from the passengers, who declare that it is hardly fair, as the dessert is often the most lingering and delightful portion of the meal.

At Bantry a large stage waits to take us to Glengariffe. Fourteen passengers beside ourselves "pile in," and away we go. The road wanders through some pretty scenery, now loitering along the bank of a mirror-like lake, now winding up the mountain side, till at last we halt before Roche's Hotel at Glengariffe. Of course we have had wet and dismal weather during the whole ride, and even now it is still raining.

The hotel is clean and attractive in all its surroundings, and we find many pleasant people here. Although it rains, and the ground is not very agreeable for walking, we cannot stay in, for we long to explore the loveliness for which this place is noted; so, protecting ourselves against the weather, we sally forth upon the path directly in front of the hotel, which faces the lake. As we stand beside this water, which is a miniature of beauty, we hear the plashing of a fall, and inquire of some boys standing by where it is. They all, and there are six of them, volunteer to guide us to it. We assent gladly, and soon find ourselves in the midst of a picturesque scene. These walks should be named Lovers' Walks, for here Nature has done her utmost to render these secluded bowers enchanting in color and environment. We wander along this charming bank until we come to a romantic little bridge, poised high up in the mountain, fully thirty feet above the water, which flows under it to the greater fall.

We leave with reluctance this delightful spot, this lovely glen, where all is serene and full of rest and peace, but on the morrow we start early in the morning for Killarney, a journey of forty-two miles, to be accomplished by stage.

"We leave with reluctance this Delightful Spot"

The Irish have great faith in the superstition associating St. Swithin with the rains at this time of the year. This is the legend:

St. Swithin, Bishop of Winchester, when dying, requested to be buried in the churchyard of the Minster, that "the sweet rain of heaven might fall upon his grave." Later, when he was canonized, the monks thought to honor the saint by removing his body into the choir, and the 15th of July was set for the ceremony; but it rained on that day, and for forty days afterwards, so violently that the monks gave up their design as contrary to the will of Heaven, and instead of removing the body, they showed their veneration by erecting a chapel over his grave. Hence the adage, "If it rains on St. Swithin's Day it will rain for forty days." As the forty days will end on the 24th of the month, it is predicted that we shall soon have fine weather. We would love dearly to see a clear day in Ireland.

From Roche's we are driven in a trap to Eccles' Hotel, where we take the "coach and four" for Killarney. There are sixteen other passengers for the same destination.

The signal is given, the driver cracks his whip, and off we go in fine style. It is unfortunate that the day is rainy, as this will spoil much of our anticipated pleasure in the landscape around us. The horses go well, the party is a jolly one, and the driver entertains us with stories and droll speeches in answer to our many questions. We pass many interesting places as we ride merrily along; among them Lord Bantry's demesne at Glengariffe, and as the road ascends, in spite of the rain, we have glimpses of magnificent scenery. Here, too, are quaint pictures of country life; and here are men driving pigs and horses, evidently on their way to market. Here is a picturesque church in a pretty bit of landscape.

Several wagons drawn by "jacks," or donkeys, appear, each wagon containing one or two women and five or six children, beside the driver, and in every case the "jack" takes the trick as the cleanest of the party.

"We pass through a Tunnel."

Most of the houses on the roadside are built of stone, but only one here and there is attractive or interesting. Now we pass through a tunnel cut through a picturesque portion of the mountain, and this proves to be the first of a series of three, each surpassing the former in romantic and beautiful surroundings. There is a great halloo and shouting as we pass in and out of these tunnels, responded to by mocking shouts and laughter from our invisible friend, the echo. We climb higher and higher, until we have attained an altitude of 1500 feet. A magnificent view here meets our eyes. Although it is raining, and there is a mist on the mountain top, we can see enough of the extensive prospect to excite our enthusiasm to the highest degree, and exclamations of "Magnificent!" "Superb!" "Sublime!" and the like are heard on all sides. Yonder is a little house nestling snugly on the mountain side, well sheltered from the cold winds of winter and the severe storms of summer. We ascend the mountains, sometimes ride long distances on the summit, and descend on the opposite side. Though the people of this section of the country may possess little of worldly wealth, here are roads that should make old Philadelphia blush with shame. There is not a rut or hole visible anywhere.

Time passes swiftly in social converse, and many of the passengers relate interesting experiences of their sojourn in foreign lands. Shortly after twelve o'clock we reach Kenmare, where we are allowed three-quarters of an hour for lunch. As we alight, we see the words " Hotel and Restaurant" over the windows of a very modest-looking house. Here, then, we must satisfy our hunger. The meal is abundant of its kind, but there is much confusion, in consequence of the demands of all the guests to be waited upon at once, and we all start in to help ourselves. However, order prevails in a short time, and the good-natured Irish lasses pass the fried eggs, chops, ham, potatoes and other viands speedily around the table.

"A MAGNIFICENT VIEW MEETS OUR EYES"

The little town of Kenmare is pleasantly situated on a bay which some one has said is the most beautiful in all Ireland ; but we have not time to explore its charming surroundings, for at one o'clock we must climb up to our places on the coach and proceed on our journey.

We have now accomplished about twenty miles, nearly half the distance between Glengariffe and Killarney. The clouds lift from time to time and give us fleeting glimpses of this wild and beautiful country. Altogether it is a most delightful ride.

We pass three gentlemen on their wheels, probably on their way from Killarney to Glengariffe, for our driver informs us that this is a favorite route of the cyclist.

As we are ascending a mountain the clouds suddenly break away and disclose the scene below. A superb picture lies at our feet. This is Coom Dhuv, the Black Valley of Killarney. Off in the distance may be seen many streams shining at the foot of the mountain, their swish and rush rising to our ears, and sounding now near, now far away, as the breezes catch them up and bring them to us, or mingle their voices with the wild roar of the mountain torrents. This is a never-to-be-forgotten scene. Farther on the Gap of Dunloe bursts upon us. How shall I describe the wonderfully blended shades of exquisite color that here meet our eyes? It is indeed impossible. These masterpieces of God are beyond description.

At every turn new scenes of beauty appear. This gap is the famous gorge in the mountains around Killarney, and this region is the wildest and most beautiful portion of Ireland. The soul of the lover of beauty is satisfied—lakes, mountains, tranquil scenes, and weird, rugged, shadowy effects of gloomy grandeur, smiling, joyous, laughing, frolicsome moods of Nature, all pass before us in infinite and magnificent variety.

We have a full view of the Upper Lake, and see in the distance the next tunnel through which we will pass. Here our driver tells us that the

"Royal Victoria Hotel, Killarney"

mountain opposite is Eagle's Nest. It is fitly named : a noble eyry for a noble bird.

We are now on the Kenmare Road, and near the end of our journey. The Earl of Kenmare, we learn, owns large estates here and in Killarney, hence we frequently hear such names as Kenmare Castle, Kenmare Woods, etc.

At last we turn from the main road on which we have passed through Killarney, and enter the long lane on our left, which leads to the Royal Victoria Hotel, and it is five o'clock when we enter its hospitable doors.

The Gap of Dunloe—
Romantic Ireland.

The Gap of Dunloe—Romantic Ireland.

The Royal Victoria Hotel—Ross Castle—To the Gap—Kate Kearney's Cottage—Fairy Glen—Serpent Lake—St. Patrick's Cottage—Macgillicuddy's Reeks—Five Islands—The Long Range—"The Happy Family"—Shooting the Rapids—The Old Bridge—Toothache Bridge—Bricken Bridge—Devil's Island—Muckross Abbey—Colleen Bawn Rock—Torc Mountain—Limerick—The Theatre Royal—River Shannon—Kilrush.

IT is fortunate that we telegraphed for a room here, for many tourists who did not take this precaution have been turned away. The short walk in front of this hotel can hardly be surpassed in beauty. The hotel itself is very attractive, and its genial manager provides good cheer for his numerous family. In the dining-room there is a long table capable of accommodating fifty-two persons, besides the many small tables. The service is first-class.

After resting, we take a walk through a portion of the Earl of Kenmare's grounds, and wander on till we come upon the old Ross Castle, from which there is a fine view. This is a picturesque ruin, covered with ivy, the ancient home of the O'Donoghues, and filled with historical associations. There are here beautiful views on every side. It is hardly necessary to say that we were caught in a shower. Anticipating this, we are prepared for it.

To-day we rise early, for the day is fine, and we have on hand the most important excursion of Killarney—a trip to the famous Gap of Dunloe. We are to proceed by car and on foot or horseback, and wind up with a row on the lake back to our hotel. This expedition will occupy about eight hours. Our car is waiting before the hotel, and we start at ten o'clock. A drive of eleven or twelve miles brings us to the entrance of the Gap. During the latter part of this ride we are besieged by innumerable old men and women, girls and boys, who have flowers, photographs, canes and other articles for sale.

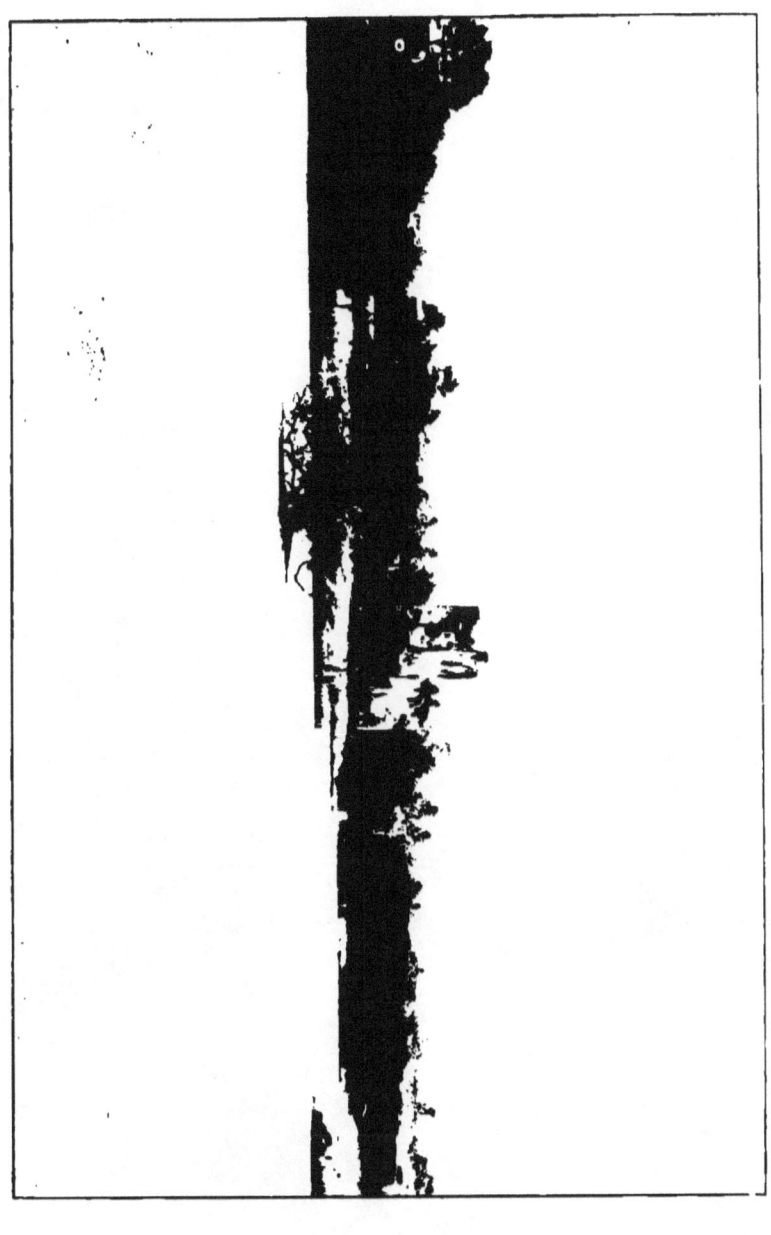

"Old Ross Castle, Killarney"

The Gap is a wild ravine through the mountains, with rocks on either side rising to an enormous height. Near the entrance an unattractive cottage is pointed out as the home of the beautiful Kate Kearney. Here one may, if he wishes, refresh himself with a drink of goat's milk. The place is so dirty, and the handmaids in charge so untidy, that we do not avail ourselves of this opportunity. Our driver now leaves us, and we find horses waiting for those who care to ride through the Gap and around the mountain to the lake where we take the boat. We are all ready, and off we start. At the very outset we are surrounded by women and girls who worry the life out of one with their importunities to buy milk, whiskey, etc. They deluge us with persuasive compliments. One old woman tells me that she has many daughters so beautiful that it would break the heart of St. Patrick himself to see them leave auld Ireland, but I am 'that fascinatin', that she will give me my choice of these fairies of the Gap.

The scene is one of great grandeur. The mountains on either side, dark, wild and barren, rise to a height of twenty-seven hundred feet. The path by which we ascend is steep and narrow. Now and then the ladies stop their horses to give us a breathing spell. When they turn to look for us they find us the centre of a group of young girls, who merrily try to sell us something to eat or drink.

No words can do justice to the scene around us. The enormous boulders and the crystal waters of the lake, each add an individual charm to our surroundings. Here is Fairy Glen, and here is Serpent Lake, where, according to tradition, St. Patrick vanquished the last snake in Ireland. The legend runs thus: When St. Patrick banished the snakes, one old serpent resisted, but the saint overcame it by cunning. He made a box and invited the serpent to enter it. The serpent insisted that it was too small, and there ensued so much contention over the matter that the serpent at last crawled into the

Fairy Glen and Serpent Lake, Gap of Dunloe

box to prove that it was right; upon which St. Patrick slammed down the lid and threw the box into the lake.

In confirmation of this legend, I may here state that we have tramped over bog and moss, and through the most tangled underbrush, without perceiving the slightest evidence of the fanged intruder in this country. Glory and honor to St. Patrick, and may no iconoclast grudge him his meed of praise.

The cottage of the Saint stands at the roadside, and here whiskey and some kinds of fruit can be purchased by the wayfarer. While resting here we hear soft sweet music, which is caught up by the echoes, and repeated over and over again in fairy-like tones. When they appear, the musicians, however, are anything but fairy-like.

We gaze long and silently at the scene. It inspires one with new thoughts to view these wonders of Nature: the massive rocks, the mountains, the lake! The intense stillness which surrounds us leaves upon the mind a strange and dreamlike impression, as of existence in another realm.

We continue the ascent until the mountain top is reached, and here we have an extensive view of the Reeks, which stretch away for miles, till the cottages seem mere specks on the mountain sides. Descending on the opposite side, we pass many simple cottages, from whose doors children run to us for pennies.

A pleasant walk of a mile or so brings us to the Upper Lake, where a large boat and two oarsmen are waiting to convey us to our hotel. We are somewhat fatigued with our five-mile tramp, and quite ready for the large hamper of good things sent to us from the hotel.

Our companions on this trip are a young vicomte and his wife, who are making their bridal tour. They are both agreeable and entertaining.

Near the lake is a very pretty cottage, formerly the property of Lord Brandon, now owned

"THE MUSICIANS, HOWEVER, ARE ANYTHING BUT FAIRY-LIKE."

The Gap of Dunloe, etc.

by Mr. Herbert, the holder of thousands of acres in this part of the country.

We are rowed slowly over the lake, passing, among others, five picturesque and celebrated islands, known as McCarthy's, Rowland's, Eagle, Duck and Juniper. These islands are covered with magnificent trees, and afford a great variety of wonderful views.

The Lakes of Killarney are set as in a bowl, in the hollow of the lofty mountains, whose bare summits are constantly swept by storms from the Atlantic. They are as a whole otherwise called Lough Lean, from being surrounded by high mountains. The trees which grow by these waters are the oak, yew, birch, hazel, mountain ash, and others, the greenest and most beautiful of all being the magnificent arbutus, which gleams out amid the forests, and haunts one with its vitality, when the tramp of the long day is done, and its pictures come back to rest with us in the twilight.

Yonder is the Purple Mountain, rising more

than twenty-seven hundred feet above the sea. Its purple effect is caused by the abundance of slate protruding from its sides, and in the sunlight it presents a truly royal appearance. On the opposite side is Torc Mountain, nearly eighteen hundred feet high. Here are Colman's Eye and Colman's Leap. Colman was once lord of the Upper Lake; in a quarrel with the O'Donoghue, being closely pursued by his adversary, he made the famous leap over the lake which has given his name to this point.

We are now on the Long Range, that beautiful body of water which connects the Upper and Lower Lakes, and which is sometimes called the Middle Lake. The mountains towering above us in their immensity make us feel our insignificance. The old boatman tells us that these mountains are called "The Happy Family," as they never fall out or have trouble.

We are under the shadow of Eagle's Nest, noted for its beautiful echo. We have no bugle to arouse the sleeping spirit of melody, but we

"We Shoot the Rapids, under Old Weir Bridge."

call forth the famous voices again and again in our own merry way, and listen to their repetitions with ever-increasing delight.

Now we are about to shoot the rapids under old Weir Bridge. There is some little excitement, although this is not a dangerous experiment, as, for instance, shooting the rapids at Niagara. We glide through the water swiftly and safely. This old bridge is said to be the most ancient one in Ireland. Tradition carries it back to mythical ages.

And here again is the "Meeting of the Waters," as they flow around Dinish Island, upon which there is a pretty little cottage for the convenience of visitors.

In the distance is a small wooden bridge, to which, we are told, is attached the superstition that whoever washes his teeth with the water that flows under it will never suffer from toothache. Of course we all make use of this wonderful remedy while passing under the bridge. If a tourist with a kodak should happen along at this moment, he might obtain a curious picture. A lady from our hotel informs me that she suffered greatly from toothache until availing herself of this prescription. Since then she has been perfectly free from it. The bridge is known as "Toothache Bridge."

This mountain scenery is wild and picturesque. Deer and rabbits abound here; also pheasants, quails and other game. The country is romantic as we approach the old Brickeen Bridge. Much has been written of the beauty of this locality, and indeed too much cannot be said in praise of any portion of this region. We are in the midst of a series of rich and varied views, of which each new one seems more charming than the last. Our hotel is now directly opposite on the Lower Lake, and four miles and a half distant.

Devil's Island is one of the many small islands around us. I do not know the origin of the name, but suppose, from the appearance of the rocks, that at some period they have been

subjected to intense heat. Perhaps they have served as a soup bowl for his satanic majesty.

At last we are at home again, at half-past five in the afternoon, a little weary in mind and body, but all declaring that this has been a " Red Letter " day, the very best we have spent since we set foot on good old Irish soil. The entire day has been clear and pleasant, a rare thing at this season.

This afternoon we make a little tour in a jaunting car, going first to Muckross Abbey in the demesne of Captain Herbert. By paying a shilling we gain admission to the beautiful grounds and the old abbey, which was founded in 1340 by the Franciscans on the site of an ancient church. There are many old tombs here, and such names as O'Sullivan, M'Carthy, O'Donoghue are frequently seen. Here is Colleen Bawn Rock, recalling to our minds the play of this name which we saw in Cork. The scene was laid in this region.

Torc Mountain is our next destination.

Before proceeding thither we have a fine view of the mountain from Dinish Cottage. Upon reaching the foot of the mountain, we are surprised to learn that we must each pay sixpence for admission. However we are becoming accustomed to this gentle reminder of the poverty of these land kings, so paying the fee, we ascend the mountain. The first object to claim our attention is the cascade, a large stream of water, leaping from its eyry and rushing with roar and foam over the broken ledges of rock, amid green trees and luxuriant foliage, to its bed among the graceful ferns below. On each side precipitous rocks, covered with luxuriant foliage, and close by on the left rises the mountain, from whose height we have a magnificent view, embracing miles upon miles of country. The distant trees and other objects appear like mere specks upon the picture.

We enjoy the fine prospect and pure atmosphere for some time, and, descending, observe the remarkable collection of natural ferns and other plants for which this spot is noted.

Golden Bawn Rock

This morning, when the hotel "bus" drives up to the door to carry passengers to the railway station, we respond regretfully to our names on the roll of those who are leaving beautiful Killarney, with its delightful walks and rides, and picturesque lakes and mountains. At 11.30 we start for Limerick, *en route* for Kilkee.

In order to take the steamer trip down the River Shannon, we remain over night at Limerick, stopping at the Glentworth Hotel, whose accommodations are only fair.

Limerick, a small place of about forty thousand souls, offers little to interest visitors. It is divided into three parts—the Irishtown, the Englishtown, and Newtown Perry, which are connected by bridges. The main street of Newtown Perry is a long and handsome one. We take a car for a short ride about the place. The old Thomond Bridge and King John's Castle are the most noteworthy objects, but our limited stay leaves us no time for them.

This evening we pay three and fivepence each,

and seat ourselves in the best seats in the balcony of the Theatre Royal, curious to see a play in old Limerick. This is the only theatre in town, and a queer place it is. The curtain rises at exactly eight o'clock, but the audience, numbering about fifty or sixty persons, makes no demonstration at this fact, the men keeping their hats on, and even smoking in the gallery above us.

The play is not badly rendered, but the orchestra amuses us more than the acting. It is composed of five would-be musicians—leader, first and second violin, pianist, cornetist, and flute player. They begin with a discord, and the leader calls to the flute player that he is not in time; then, loudly enough to be heard by the whole audience, he orders the second violin to play G sharp. Finally the discord is such that the leader stops playing and begins to tune one of his violin strings, while the other players continue their jargon of unmusical sounds. The leader frequently calls out: "One—two—three," keeping time with his bow, and trying to make them play in harmony.

This is to us the most laughable farce, while to the audience the orchestra is, without doubt, the Sousa or Gilmore Band of Limerick. The entertainment reminds me of an anecdote told me in this country. A minister invited some visitors to his church, remarking that they had a "fool" (full) choir, and that good singing might be expected. Is the Limerick orchestra also a "fool" orchestra?

This morning we bid farewell to the ancient town, and board the steamer *Shannon*, for our trip down the beautiful river which divides the counties of Limerick and Clare. The Shannon is from four to seven miles wide. It is a glorious river, broad and deep, flowing a distance of two hundred miles from its source to the sea, and watering ten Irish counties. The scenery near Limerick is very beautiful, the day is fine, and in the deep blue sky heavy white clouds form mountains upon mountains, until one could almost imagine himself viewing the Arctic regions. The captain sits beside us and tells many stories of the victims this great body of water has made of the foolhardy.

At 12.45 we reach Kilrush, the end of our voyage, and here we have two hours before taking train for Kilkee.

What an ancient and dirty-looking place this is! Here, indeed, one sees " the wide waste of all-devouring years." At the junction of three streets, about forty old men and women, dressed in rags, are selling potatoes, apples and cabbages, which are piled up in the street and quickly measured out to those who wish to purchase. The shops are dusty and dingy, and the children, with rare exceptions, look as if water is as great a stranger to them as is their good sovereign.

So we learn by comparison the progress of the different nations, and observe in its superior march in the realms of intellect, which is destined to be queen of all the nations.

*Kilkee, Galway, Clifden, Sligo,
by Rail and River.*

Kilkee, Galway, Clifden, Sligo, by Rail and River.

Kilkee—The Cliffs—Dunlicky Castle and Bishop's Island—"Evicted Houses"—The Main Street—Caves of Kilkee — Keeping the Sabbath — Galway — Eyre Square —Church of St. Nicholas—Salmon Leap—Fish Market—Salt Hill—On the Road to Clifden—The New Railroad —Rainbow—Clifden—On the Way to Westport—Letterfrack—Kylemore Castle—Leenane — Westport—Ride to Sligo—The Rapids—Ballysodare—Sligo—Lough Gill—Our Old Driver—The White Donkey—Stories by the Way—Drumcliffe Round Tower—Cliffs on the Glencar—Going for Turf—Bundoran.

TIME is up, and we are on the road to Kilkee, a distance of nine miles, which is soon accomplished. This is the end of our day's journey. We drive with our grips to Moore's Hotel, which is considered the best in the place. As we leave for Galway at half-past eight to-morrow morning, we must see as much of this town as possible in the intervening time. It faces the broad Atlantic, and is deemed one of the most charming watering-places in Ireland, being surrounded by beautiful cliff scenery.

We ride some fifteen miles in a jaunting car, around by the cliff or ocean side, and home by the banks of the Shannon. The scenery by the cliffs is most grand. One should see these rocks to appreciate them. I can give no idea in words of the impression made by the vast space below us. Seen from the steamers that pass this way, these perpendicular rocks, towering high above the water's edge, seem like giant sentinels guarding the pretty town. In winter the spray is so great that it is impossible to walk on this road, and during some of the storms it is said to be blinding.

We observe queer nooks and caves in the rocks, worn by the constant beating of the waves. The largest cave is about two miles from the town, and is best visited by boat. The entrance to it is sixty feet in height, and we are told that its interior is very beautiful.

"IN THE DISTANCE IS BISHOP'S ISLAND"

Interesting points abound in this neighborhood. As we ride we come upon a fine view of the town of Kilkee, and a charming picture it makes, with the rocks and ocean in the foreground. In the distance is Bishop's Island, with many sheep grazing on its fine pasturage. As we approach Dunlicky Castle, we note the massive strength of its walls, which have withstood the winds and storms of ages. Tradition says the mortar was mixed with cow's blood; hence its great power of adhesion.

In many places these picturesque caves run clear through the masses of rock. We pass several houses in ruins on our way back to the hotel, and are told by our driver that they are "evicted houses," the tenants having been turned out for being unable to pay the rent. On the main street some few signs of life are visible, for here are the various shops and other business places. An old farmer goes along before us with his wagon and pen of hogs, and here is another with a load of peat or turf; passing from one curious and often pitiable sight to another, we frequently exclaim: "Why do not these poor souls leave this distressed country and seek better homes in America?"

This morning, Sunday, I try to persuade an old boatman to row us through the caves of Kilkee, one especially, which is said to be grand beyond description; but he will not do so for any compensation that I may offer: "No, not for fifteen pounds," as he expresses it. I ask why there is such a superstition about going through the caves on Sunday, and am informed that many years ago there was a period when the fish seemed to shun this coast, and there was great distress among the people in consequence. The fishermen, fearing they were going to lose forever their means of livelihood, sought in a body the advice and assistance of the Catholic Church. Ten bishops were sent to Kilkee, to intercede with the Creator for the restoration of the fish to this coast. The fishermen assembled, and as the bishops besought the Lord to return

Main Road, Galway

to these poor souls their only means of subsistence as in past years, the men solemnly promised to keep the Sabbath in holy reverence forever. From that day, it is said, God restored their treasure, and the fishermen have kept their vow. Nothing can induce them to move one jot on the Sabbath.

We leave Kilkee on the morning train for Ennistymon, thence, in consequence of heavy rains, we proceed by rail to Galway, although our plan was to travel from Ennistymon to Ballyvaughan by jaunting car, and take the steamer over the bay to Galway. So we journey via Athenry to Galway, arriving at 2.30 p. m., and take up our quarters at Mack's Royal Hotel. As usual, we start out almost immediately in a jaunting car, to view the sights of the town. There is much to interest us here. Galway presents a strange mixture of poverty and prosperity. There are many untenanted and ruined houses here, while in the main streets there are new and fine-looking shops, new thoroughfares being opened up, and modern villas erected in the suburbs. Here and there we see traces of Spanish architecture in odd gate-ways and square court-yards. Eyre Square, in the heart of the town, is a large enclosure, laid out in walks, and planted with trees, and close by is the church of St. Nicholas, in a corner of which is the notable tablet commemorating that Warden of Galway who, according to tradition, assisted at the execution of his own son. This is a fine old building, containing some interesting monuments, and a picturesque view of the town and its environments may be seen from its steeple.

Lynch's Castle, in Shop Street, is one of those ancient dwellings, whose fine and curious sculpture and noble coat of arms evince the former grandeur of this place. The ground floor is a grocery store, the windows and doors are ornamented with rich carving, and upon the roof are gargoyles to throw off the water. These quaint buildings and the primitive ways of some of the people render this a delightful place to visit.

"We have never seen their like before."

We pass several boat clubs, among them the Royal Club; and here is the Salmon Leap, where the fish are caught in great numbers with line and net. The old fishermen may be seen at the fish market at Salt Hill. On our way thither we pass the steamer which runs across Galway Bay. It is called *The Citie of Tribes.*

Before we reach Salt Hill, which faces the bay, we come to the Claddagh, close by the harbor, which is inhabited by a purely Celtic population, numbering about four thousand. They are all fishermen, and it is impossible to conceive of a more curious, ancient-looking place. People, houses, everything connected with this spot seem old, excepting the fish exposed for sale.

The town is composed of miserable cabins of mud and stone, the great number of them windowless. They are now having a fish sale, and it is an odd sight. I have obtained a few photographs of these typical old folk of Ireland. They are so interesting to us that I fear we transgress all the rules of etiquette in our wondering observation, for we have never seen their like before.

It is the hour at which the long jaunting car leaves Galway for Clifden, a journey of fifty-two miles. Bidding farewell to this peculiar place, we start off with six other passengers.

The gentleman and lady beside us are Glasgow people, from whom we learn much regarding routes, etc., which will prove useful when travelling in their country. Our car is the mail car. A railroad between Galway and Clifden was finished only six weeks ago, but as the contract with the coach line has not yet expired, the latter still carries the mail between the two cities. As we plod along in our primitive way, we hear the shrill whistle of a locomotive, and see the train speeding over the new road, and, viewing the two modes of travel, the old and the new, I am impressed with the perseverance and progress of man, in pushing capital into quarters so firmly stamped with the spirit of antediluvianism.

The road is exceptionally good, though hilly

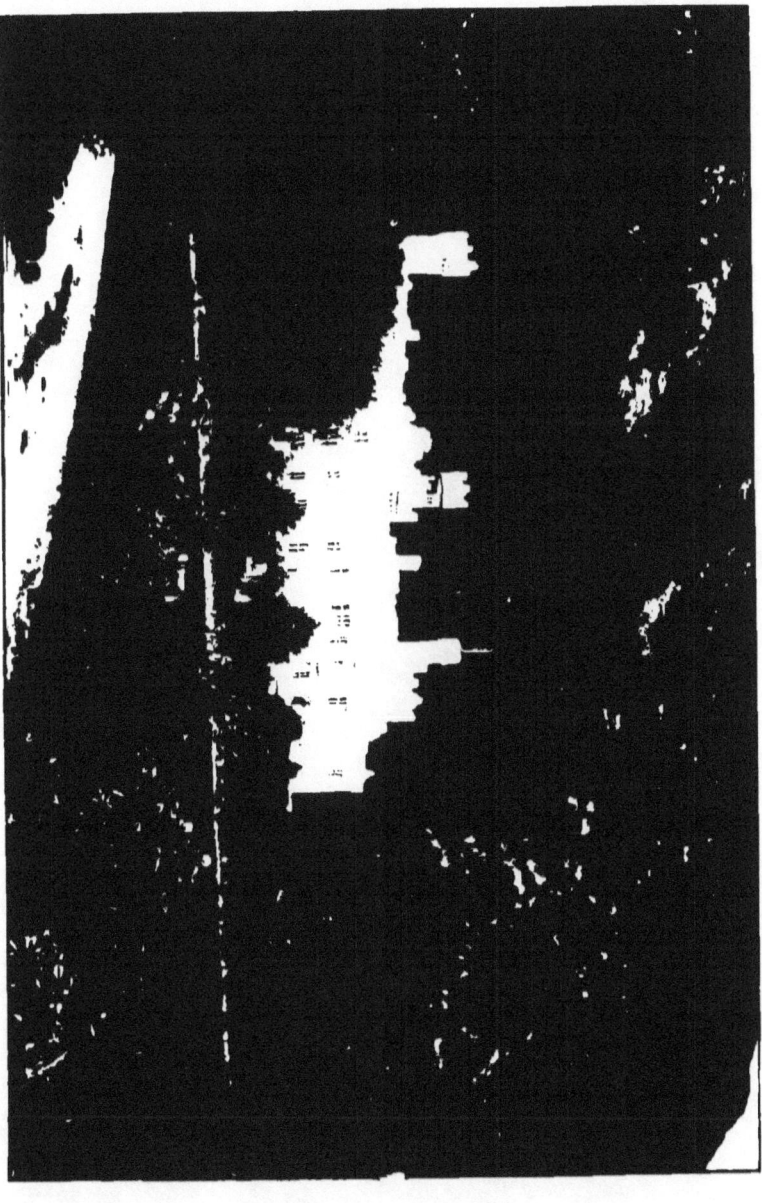

"We find ourselves within sight of the beautiful and picturesque Kylemore Castle"

in places. We are surprised at the great quantity of stone in this region. Field after field, for many miles, is filled with this serious obstacle to agriculture. Here is a long deep cut, through which the new railroad passes. The scenery along the whole route is picturesque and full of interest. At times the rain comes down, dampening our ardor somewhat, but taking it altogether we are as jolly and happy as though the sun was master of the situation.

Ahead of us loom the " Twelve Pins," a grand collection of tall mountain peaks on either side of the road. At this point the sun peeps out for a few moments, and its reflection on the mist forms one of the most perfectly arched rainbows that I have ever seen. It is in blocks of pure color, as though one has taken his brush and painted solid lines of blue, green, yellow and red.

So many lovely scenes pass before us that the eye is almost wearied by the constant succession of picturesque views.

The day is raw and chilly, and, though it is anti-temperance, one finds a little " nip " very comforting in the face of a wet ride, but we reach Clifden in time for a good hot supper at Mullarkey's Hotel, and soon " Richard's himself again."

In Clifden itself there is little to interest the stranger. It is built at the centre of " one of those numerous indentations in the land which give the name Connamara, that is, Bays of the Sea." At the back of the town rise the mountains, while in front is the Bay of Ardbear, and beyond, the Atlantic Ocean. Yet we could pass a few days here very happily had we the time. Clifden Castle is a rather fine-looking building, modern in style, standing in the valley among sheltering trees, and here the scene is one of great beauty. The cliffs overlooking the bay tempt us to linger within sight of the boundless sea and purple hills.

We are called at seven this morning, for we are to breakfast at eight, as our car leaves at

"We take our places in the large jaunting car that leaves for Sligo."

nine o'clock sharp for Westport, some forty-two miles distant. The day is damp and there is so much mist that we all fear there is rain ahead, but the ride is fine, in spite of these disadvantages. We make a short stop at Letterfrack, a small village, pretty, neat and comfortable looking, which, it is said, owes its prosperity to the Society of Friends, who have reclaimed a great part of the surrounding country.

Now we come to a wild mountain pass, where the rocks are piled up to a great height, and in many places jut far out over the road. There is a dense growth of trees extending from base to summit. Soon after we find ourselves within sight of the beautiful and picturesque Kylemore Castle, the residence of Mr. Mitchell Henry. The scene here is superb. The lake lies in front of the handsome structure, while in the background are lofty and precipitous mountains. Nothing can be more romantic. The mountains about here are fully two thousand feet high. The illustration shows the castle as seen from our car. The picture is one which cannot soon be forgotten.

For many miles the road is bounded by hedges made of fuchsias. At one o'clock we stop at Leenane, where we are allowed a half hour for dinner. There is a cosy little hotel here, and we soon find provisions to which we do ample justice. Fresh horses are put in, and we are away again along the road amid fine and extensive views. We follow Lake Killery for many miles, now and then seeing a fisherman hauling in his net or fishing from a boat. The wild and rugged aspect of the neighboring mountains imparts a grandeur to this portion of the country which is wholly its own. At times it rains quite fast; then the clouds seem to lighten, and we have hopes of clearing weather. But these hopes are not fulfilled; it rains during the remainder of the journey.

What a damp party we are: wraps, coats, gloves, hats, umbrellas, everything, dripping as we draw up before the spacious Railway Hotel at

"Picturesque Mountains are on our Right"

Westport. The rooms in this hotel are utterly disproportionate in size, what they call a "large" room being twenty feet by sixty, while the "small" ones are six feet by ten (why, the Irish architect alone knows). When asked which kind of a room we wish, we inquire if there is not a happy medium that we can have, between the two. But this is impossible, so we content ourselves with the "large" chamber. It seems wild and "eerie," and throughout the night

>"a thousand fantasies
>Begin and throng into my memory,
>Of calling shapes and beckoning shadows dire,
>And airy tongues that syllable men's names,
>And sands, and shores, and desert wildernesses."

Westport is an uninteresting town, and we do not wish to remain here longer than is necessary to recover from the fatigue of the long ride from Clifden. We take the Midland Great Western Railway for Ballina, and arriving there in due time, proceed to Moy's Hotel. After lunching, we take our places in the large jaunting car that leaves for Sligo, forty-six English miles distant. This is a delightful ride. Many picturesque mountains are on our right, while on the left we have charming glimpses of the ocean.

This northern section of the country is under better cultivation, and the soil is much richer than the southern districts. Here are many pigs, " the gentlemen who pay the rent." Now and then I jump off the car and walk. The road is very interesting, as one after another, the milestones on our left appear and vanish in the distance. Our horses, though slow, are sure, and although there are clouds, we have no rain— which is a blessing.

Passing over a small bridge, and making a turn in the road, we come upon the Rapids Ballysodare which fall into the bay over a series of rocky ledges, forming a beautiful picture. In the distance we behold the town of Sligo and a portion of Lough Gill.

Some of these Irish towns present lovely views as we approach them. The different

"We have an old driver, full of Irish wit and history"

church spires, rising above the other buildings, silently impress one with the Christian atmosphere of the community. Crossing the old Sligo Bridge, we drive through Knox Street, and at last halt before the Imperial Hotel. A rather attractive hall meets our eyes; rooms are assigned us, and after a good supper, we retire for the night.

The regular mail jaunting car leaves Sligo at 6.30 a. m. and at 3 p. m. One hour is too early, the other too late for us, so our accommodating host engages a private car to take us to Bundoran, twenty-three miles distant. The fare for a small one-horse car is sixpence à mile. We start off with all our traps at ten o'clock. It is a magnificent day. While clouds float in the sky, they form themselves into beautiful effects, and there is enough blue to make several pairs of trousers, so we are confident that the weather will favor us. The prospect is beautiful, both near and distant. Majestic mountains, rising to wonderful heights, impress us more and more with the supreme power of the Heavenly Father, who sustains and beautifies His creations for the joy of His children.

While the country engages our attention, it does not monopolize it, for we have an old driver, full of Irish wit and history.

"On every point, in earnest or in jest
 His judgment and his prudence and his wit
Were deem'd the very touchstone, and the test
 Of what was proper, graceful, just and fit."

He more than answers all our questions. What a success he would be in America as the serio-comic man. On the way we pass a field in which a white donkey is grazing.

"That donk'," he says, pointing to it, "is a fortunate baste."

"Why so?" is asked.

"Well," says the old driver, "do you see that house on the fir hill?"

We see it.

"In that house lived an old man, who all his life had a great likin' for that white donk'. About

"WE PASS MANY CHILDREN ON DONKEYS, WITH BASKETS ON EITHER SIDE, GOING FOR TURF."

two year ago the old man died, and, would ye belave it, he willed a pace of ground to the old donk'. Yes, ye can see it on yer left. That field is to be the donk's as long as Mr. Donk lives. And from that day to this, I have passed that white donk', and never a bit of work have I seen him do, an' shure I'm tellin' yez the truth."

So he goes on from one story to another, sometimes relating events that happened " over yon," when he was a boy. " Ha! ha! ha! Shure, I must tell yez of the time when we had the big blow on yonder mountain. I was walkin' along one morning when I met old Paddy O'Hea. Sez Paddy, sez he: ' Good mornin', Dan.'

"Sez I to Paddy: 'Good mornin' to yez.' An' Paddy sez, ' It's a good mornin',' an' sez I to Paddy, ' It's a lyin' yer after.'

"Then Paddy sez to me: ' Did ye hear the news, Dan?'

"' In faith, I did not, when I was not there.'

" Sez Paddy: ' It was a smart blow we were havin' last night.'

"Sez I: 'Faith, I know that.'

"'The roof of the old mill blowed off,' sez Paddy.

"'The divil,' sez I. 'Yes,' says Paddy.

"'Ha! ha! ha! Shure, what are ye given' me?' sez I.

"'An',' sez Paddy: 'Ha! ha! ha! Did ye know old Johnny O'Toole?'

"'Well did I.'

"'Johnny was on top of his hay poil in the field, when the wand caught the poil o' hay, an' carried Johnny two mile yon.'

"'Och,' sez I, 'It's lyin' ye are.'

"'In faith it's thrue,' sez Paddy. 'Ha! ha! ha! Them was great days.'"

His stories are numberless, and we are so well entertained that the time passes quickly.

Here is Drumcliffe with its beautiful round tower, a historic ruin. There is very fine scenery here, with the sea on one side and the mountains on the other. As we approach the Cliffs on the Glencar, the brilliant effect of the sun on the

"There are many 'odd sights'"

rocks is very striking. We pass many children on donkeys, with baskets on either side, going for turf. The picture on the opposite page is a truthful representation of what one often sees in this section of the country. There are many odd sights, but all are interesting. Ofttimes a small cart drawn by a donkey will go by, with Paddy and his old lady comfortably enjoying their drive. And, so we ride on and on, until our driver points out the town of Bundoran, and we are both glad and sorry that our journey has come to an end, for the day is delightful, the country charming, and our driver has done his best to enliven the way.

Famous Irish Towns and Their Industries

The Giant's Causeway

Famous Irish Towns and their Industries— The Giant's Causeway.

Bundoran—Along the Cliffs—Ballyshannon—Falls of Erne—Belleek Pottery—Lough Erne—Crevinish Castle—Devenish Abbey and Round Tower—Enniskillen—Londonderry—Lough Swilly—The Old Wall—Portrush—The Giant's Causeway—Recognizing a Philadelphian—The Organ—Honeycomb—Loom—Lord Antrim's Parlor—The Fan—Keystone—Ladies' Wishing Chair—Old Women—The Chimneys—The Well—The Giant's Eyeglass—Dunluce Castle—Belfast—The Wanamaker of Belfast—Royal Damask Linen Factory—Ormeau Park—Cave Hill—Irish Hospitality.

OUR destination is the Great Northern Hotel, which is a short distance from the town. We arrive at ten minutes past one, having been three hours and ten minutes on the way. Our room faces the Atlantic, and if our eyes could penetrate the space between, they might look upon the dear ones at home, for a straight line stretched across this vast distance, would, I believe, touch the neighborhood of those we love.

After luncheon, we wander about the extensive grounds of the hotel. Here we see ladies and gentlemen playing golf, which is the first time we have witnessed the game in this country. The views from the hotel are beautiful. In the foreground is the broad Atlantic, and on every other side mountains upon mountains form scenes of great grandeur. The popular walks are along the cliffs, where many a lovely picture is seen at every turn. The sea is quite turbulent at many points along the base of the cliffs, the waters foaming and dashing against the rocks with such force that they rebound as though shot from a cannon's mouth. We are enraptured with this varied and enchanting prospect.

"I'm not romantic but upon my word,
   There are some moments when one can't help
      feeling

GREAT NORTHERN HOTEL, BUNDORAN

>   As if his heart's chords were so strongly stirr'd
>   By things around him, that 'tis vain concealing,
>   A little music in his soul still lingers,
>   Whene'er its keys are touched by Nature's fingers."

A trip has been proposed, by jaunting car to Belleek, thence by a small steamer down Lough Erne to Enniskillen, returning to Bundoran by train. We start this morning at eleven o'clock, passing through the old village of Ballyshannon, a quaint-looking place, where we see many of the people going about barefooted. Here we see the beautiful and picturesque Falls of Erne. After a delightful drive of eight miles, we find ourselves at Belleek, famous for its pottery. Thither we proceed at once, as we wish to observe the process of manufacturing this noted and delicate ware. A young man at the door invites us to enter. He also kindly acts as our guide, and we pass an interesting hour and a half in a tour through the various departments.

We see first the natural clay, then the refined

clay, and the rooms in which the different kinds of clay are ground and mixed. We walk through the department where cups, saucers, plates, pitchers, bowls and vases are moulded and turned upon a lathe in rapid succession: also that in which flowers and other curious ornaments, shells, horns and a variety of designs are shaped. How skilful these workmen are in moulding the many different patterns. In the Painting Room the most delicate tints of all the colors of the rainbow are reproduced, as well as the most brilliant hues. Now we are before the firing ovens in which the ware is hardened, and now in the Glazing Room, and so on until we are bewildered with the intricate manipulations of the process.

Across the street is a clean comfortable hotel in which we are served with a good dinner before proceeding to the steamboat landing for our sail down Lough Erne. The day is cloudy, but delightful. We have some showers, but one expects these in this country. At 3.15, we board the steamboat, and start on a twenty-two

mile excursion down the Lough. Exquisite scenes greet us on right and left. Here is Crevinish Castle, ancient and picturesque; and here are the ruins of the old Devenish Abbey, and close by the Round Tower, said to be the most perfect of its kind in the kingdom, set like jewels upon green Devenish Island, and finally round a turn in the lough, Enniskillen bursts upon us in all its beauty. This town is built upon an island in the river connecting the Upper and Lower Loughs Erne, and partly on the main-land with which it is connected by two bridges. There are many objects of interest in this romantic neighborhood, and the town is well worth a much longer visit than our time allows.

We observe a number of good buildings, two forts commanding the pass across the river, and the remains of the gate-way of an old castle. The situation of the place is ideal, and we leave it with reluctance to take the train back to Bundoran. This has been altogether a most charming day.

Bundoran is a delightful place, and we are sorry to leave it. We have made pleasant friends here, among them an interesting Irish gentleman and his wife, who urge us to spend some time with them at their home. We arrive at Jury's Hotel, Londonderry, this afternoon, and after engaging our room, take the car for Buncrana, a watering-place on Lough Swilly, about an hour's ride from here.

This is a very pretty place, surrounded by cultivated fields and trees, with a background of hills, rugged, gray and wild. From the remaining tower of its ruined castle are magnificent views of the Lough and the surrounding country. Lough Swilly extends thirty miles inland from the Atlantic, and is almost entirely surrounded by land. Returning to Londonderry, we walk around the old wall, from which we have a good view of all parts of the city. From the Walker monument we also have an extensive prospect. A cannon protruding from a port-hole in the Round Tower bears the date 1590. London-

"EXQUISITE SCENES GREET US ON RIGHT AND LEFT"

derry is famous for its successful resistance to the siege of James II. This siege lasted one hundred and five days, during which, writes an historian, the people were reduced to the direst extremities. The town is situated upon the Foyle River, which is here crossed by a handsome bridge twelve hundred feet in length. It is quite a modern-looking place, with many large buildings, and much trade, for it manufactures linen in large quantities, and possesses besides, ship-building yards, iron foundries, distilleries and breweries.

At breakfast this morning we meet an agreeable Philadelphia lawyer, the first Philadelphian we have been fortunate enough to meet since leaving home. We became acquainted in this wise: When I heard my neighbor ask some one near him to pass him the "preserves," I smiled and said to him: "You are a Philadelphian." He answered in the affirmative, laughing heartily at my means of recognizing a fellow-citizen. None but Philadelphians ever use the word "preserves" in speaking of conserved fruit.

We rise in time for another stroll through the city this morning. Lough Foyle, into which the river flows, more than half surrounds the hill upon which this town is built; the summit of the hill forms a large square, from which the principal streets diverge at right angles. From the opposite side of the river, there is a very attractive view of the city. A few of the ancient houses with high gables still exist, but they have been altered in many respects, and are not good specimens of the old-fashioned residences. There is a spacious harbor, and regular communication by water with Glasgow and several English ports.

From Londonderry we go on to Portrush, arriving at one o'clock. We have our baggage sent to the Railway Hotel, while we secure seats in the electric tram-car for the Giant's Causeway, three-quarters of an hour's ride from here. This electric tram-way is the first of its kind constructed in the United Kingdom. It was opened by Lord Spencer, September, 1883.

We are accompanied on this expedition by

"Port Coon Cave"

our friend from Philadelphia and his travelling companion, and we are a lively and congenial party, as we sally forth with our guide to see all that is to be seen. First of all luncheon is in order. After this the guide leads us to the foot of the cliffs, where we engage a boat and two sturdy oarsmen to row us into Port Coon Cave and around the Causeway. The day is fine, and while the ocean is not smooth, it is calm enough to admit of our going into the cave. Here copper, lead and other minerals glisten through the rocks, and the waves dashing wildly against the walls do not add to our feeling of safety in this subterranean region. We spend about an hour rowing about, and take a view of the famous Causeway from the water before landing. It appears to be an enormous hill of basalt, composed of nearly perpendicular columns, cut in two by a vertical section, and the half next the sea carried away. It extends a vast distance along the coast, and is from three to four hundred feet high. The name Causeway has been given it in consequence of the immense pavement, as it were, which is formed by the upper edges of the fragments of basalt left here at the bottom of the huge precipice when the seaward half of the basaltic hill was carried away. This pavement has been traced into the ocean as far as the eye can see in a clear and calm day. There are three of the pavements, the Great Causeway, the Middle Causeway and the West Causeway.

We tread upon this most marvellous formation, and as we proceed our wonder increases with every step. Here are columns fitted so closely together, that although each is perfectly distinct, it is impossible to insert the smallest thing between them. There are myriads of these columns composed of short lengths articulated into each other, as a ball into a socket. They are as smooth as if polished and carefully placed by human hands, and are five, six, seven, eight and even nine-sided.

Before us is a mass of basaltic pillars, with the longest in the middle, gradually shortening

"View of the Famous Causeway".

towards the sides as the pipes of the organ, from which it has received its name. Here is the Honeycomb, and new wonders follow each other in rapid succession. Now the fluted columns of the Loom rise up forty or fifty feet, and as straight as arrows. Now we are in Lord Antrim's Parlor, and here is before us the Fan formed by Nature's hand. This is the Keystone, and farther on, most important of all, is the Ladies' Wishing Chair, with its legend that whoever wishes within its charmed enclosure will have her (or his) desire fulfilled within the year. Of course we all take advantage of this great opportunity. I wonder how many of our wishes will come true.

Surrounding the Chair are many old women, who shower blessings upon us, and in return expect us to buy the various articles they have for sale. In the midst of these interesting objects, we look up and see a mass of rock shooting far beyond the main body, and much resembling its namesake, the Chimneys.

Another short walk brings us to the Wishing

Well, with its tradition similar to that of the Ladies' Chair. We all drink of the water, and now are doubly spellbound, with a rich prospect before us. Here is the Giant's Eyeglass, an oblong hole extending quite through the solid rock. A peculiarity of this giant is that he wears no glass in his *pince-nez*.

Legends innumerable attach themselves to this remarkable spot. It would be impossible to give one half of them. I will merely relate the most widely-spread tradition regarding the origin of the Causeway.

Fin MacCool, giant and champion of Ireland, became greatly incensed by the insolent boasting of a certain Caledonian giant, who vowed he would vanquish any one who dared to meet him, and who boldly declared that if it were not for the wetting, he would swim over and give Fin himself a good drubbing. This was too much for the Irish champion, who applied to the king, and obtained permission to construct a causeway over the watery space. The Scot walked over

"SURROUNDING THE CHAIR ARE MANY OLD WOMEN"

and fought the Irishman, and Fin was the victor. With Hibernian generosity he invited his former rival to marry and settle down in the auld country, which the Caledonian was not loath to do, as at that time living in Scotland was none of the best, and every one knows that Ireland was the richest country in the world. When the days of the giants were over, the causeway fell into disuse, and sank under the sea, leaving only a portion visible here, a little at Rathlin Island, ten miles off the coast, and the portals of the grand gate on the Island of Staffa.

The cave, it is said, was inhabited by a hermit giant, who, having made a vow never to eat food touched by human hands, was sustained by the seals, who brought him the means of nourishment in their mouths.

On the homeward ride we pass many interesting basaltic formations, and many relics of the Irish Champion. Here we have Fin's Punch-Bowl, his face in profile; also his grandmother, the Giant's Head, the Elephant, the White Rocks, etc. There are innumerable caves of various shapes, and we feel that we could spend long days exploring the wonders of this most marvellous region. Here upon an isolated rock rising steeply over a hundred feet above the sea is Dunluce Castle. It is a roofless ruin, covered with vines, accessible only by a narrow bridge raised high above the water. Its history is lost in the mists of the ages, but it is the subject of innumerable legends and romances. Beneath the rock upon which it stands is a cavern, accessible from the sea only at low water.

On the outskirts of Portrush we perceive many bathers enjoying their dip in the sea. There seems to be much entertainment here, and the waving handkerchiefs and merry voices give evidence of the exhilarating effects of the salt water. And now we are nearing our hotel. Before he leaves us our guide tells us that upwards of a thousand tourists have been known to visit the Causeway in a single day. So popular is Ireland's greatest wonder. To-morrow, if all is favorable, we move onward to Belfast, where we hope to mingle a little rest with our sight-seeing. The wise man remembers the claims of the body and brain while travelling, for at such times the tax on both is great.

Before leaving this attractive spot, we take a jaunting car and ride around the town, and far out into the suburbs. Portrush is a fashionable watering-place, hence the better class of English and Irish people is well represented here. There is a fine beach here for bathing, and numerous pleasant villas and other buildings of no mean pretensions. There are churches of all denominations to be seen. The scenery along the cliffs is fine, and the views from the headlands is most beautiful.

We are on the train, the bell rings, and off we start for Belfast. The country around us is very pretty. Farms are under cultivation, and there are signs of order and prosperity everywhere. We arrive at Belfast after a delightful journey, and drive to the Grand Central Hotel, a new house, and the finest in the place. It is situated on Royal Avenue.

Belfast, the headquarters of the linen trade, is a cheerful place, and its dwellings have a comfortable, prosperous appearance. In the suburbs are many fine villas. The city is full of the vigor and bustle of an American town. There are many good-looking churches, and we are favorably impressed with the architecture of the public buildings and the remarkable cleanliness of the streets. We visit the store of Messrs. Robinson & Cleaver, the Wanamaker's of Belfast. This is a great shop. Here is a fine display of goods, including linens of every kind and size, at astonishingly low prices when compared with those in our own city. It is unnecessary to say that we indulged to some extent in these rare fabrics.

Being interested in the hand looms and the old linen factories, we proceed by tram to the mill of Messrs. Murphy & Orr, on the outskirts of the city, with a letter of introduction from these gentlemen to their foreman. Here we are pleasantly received, and conducted through the old mill, which has been in existence eighty years. Everything is explained to our utmost satisfaction. We pass many other large linen factories on the way thither.

Saturday being a half holiday, mills and shops are closed at twelve or one o'clock, but we are in time for a number of the stores, which we find very attractive. This afternoon we take a car for a tour of the city and out into the suburbs. We see many fine residences, churches, colleges and other institutions.

The grounds of Ormeau Park are very beautiful. This was originally the demesne of the Marquis of Donegal. It was purchased by the city in 1870. Parties of ladies and gentlemen are playing tennis, cricket and other games. Some are engaged in bowls. Here is a fine bowling-green. We pass the Institute for the Deaf and Dumb, and the Royal Botanic Gardens, which are romantically situated on the

Laggan River, and contain the most beautiful flower-beds I have ever seen. Queen's College is a handsome building, six hundred feet long, with a tower a hundred feet in height. The president of this college is the Rev. Henry Cooke, for thirty years the acknowledged leader of the Conservative Party in the north of Ireland.

Cave Hill is three miles north of the city, and twelve hundred feet above the level of the sea. It derives its name from three caves beneath its surface. The view from the summit is very fine. From this eminence may be seen the town of Belfast and its spacious bay; also Belfast Castle, a baronial mansion of the Marquis of Donegal. Many elegant residences are in this neighborhood. After visiting the vast ship-yards of Messrs. Harlan & Wolff, we return to our hotel over Queen's Bridge, a most picturesque structure, spanning the river not far from the terminus of the County Down Railway, with five arches of fifty feet span each. This evening we attend the Belfast Exhibition, a small show and not very interesting.

Sunday we rest and visit Belfast friends, for to-morrow we leave for Stranraer, Scotland, via Larne. The days now are full of sunshine, with scarcely any rain.

I cannot bid farewell to Ireland without a tribute to the warm hospitality of a noble Irish gentleman, whose wife and daughter we met at Bundoran. These ladies insisted upon our visiting the husband and father at their home in Belfast, and accordingly wrote, requesting him to call upon us on our arrival in the city. On Saturday morning Mr. W. appeared at our hotel, and escorted us to many interesting places in the neighborhood, and at parting, invited us to dine with him on the following day.

We had a most delightful visit. The home of our friend is on a fine estate in the suburbs, where we found a spacious mansion, extensive lawns and beautiful grounds. At the entrance to the long avenue our host met us with a cordial welcome. We dined at three, and afterwards feasted upon luscious grapes from his hothouses. Then the carriage was brought around, and Mr. W. and his sister took us through a picturesque portion of the country, Mr. W. himself driving the fine spirited horses. We were out about two hours; on our return tea was served, and we were not allowed to leave until the old clock in the hall struck seven. Such genuine hospitality to utter strangers has made a deep and lasting impression upon us. Here we have seen what is far beyond the beauties of scenery—the warm open heart of the true Irish gentleman.

The Land of Burns—

Glasgow—The Trossachs.

The Land of Burns—Glasgow—The Trossachs.

Larne—Stranraer—The Land of Burns—Ayr—Burns' Cottage—The Monument—Relics of the Poet—Pictures—Glasgow—Origin of the Name—Royal Princess Theatre—About the City—The Cathedral—West End Park—James Watt—The Clyde—Loch Lomond—The Trossachs—Inversnaid—Loch Katrine—Rob Roy's Hut—Stronachlachar—Ellen's Isle—Our Coach—Loch Ard.

WE leave Belfast on the 9.05 train, and reach Larne at 10 o'clock. There is a delightful view of Lough Larne from the car window. Many pleasure-boats may be seen on this placid body of water. The town is beautifully situated, and like most of the old places here, has its ruined castle, which was at one time an important defensive fortress. But we have little time for observation, as we make close connection with the steamship line here, and our luggage is quickly transferred to the

Princess May, from whose deck we bid farewell to good old Ireland.

The water is somewhat rough, and in a short time the spray drives us to the shelter of the cabin. Many passengers are sea-sick. While the sea air is delightful, we are enveloped in a fog, which is by no means pleasant. We reach our destination in a few hours, no doubt to the joy of the others as well as ourselves. On the steamer we make the acquaintance of a young lawyer from Edinburgh, who invites us cordially to visit his family. It is very pleasant to experience such delightful hospitality. We are welcomed everywhere, and often feel that we are among dear old friends.

The distance from Larne to Stranraer is thirty-nine miles. This town owes its name to a visit from St. Patrick, who is said to have *stepped across* from Ireland one day. It appears to be a prosperous place. A large park of several thousand acres surrounds the residence of the Earl of Stair, and within this park are the ruins of Castle

Kennedy on slightly elevated ground between two large lochs. Its pleasure-grounds are preserved in the ancient style, with avenues, groups of plantations, shrubberies, open lawns and sloping terraces. It is said to be a favorite resort of tourists. Many rare trees and plants are to be found here, and the pinetum, extending over twenty acres, is one of the finest collections of coniferous trees in Europe.

We go by train from Stranraer to Glasgow, stopping at Ayr, the birthplace of Burns, which place we reach at half-past two in the afternoon. We find comfortable quarters at the Station Hotel, and after lunching are ready to jump into the landau ordered for a tour of the town. Ayr is on the sea-coast, at the mouth of the Ayr River, and is well laid out. In the Square near the station is a statue of Burns. A few fragments of the fort of Ayr, built by Cromwell in 1652, still remain, also an old tower which has been remodelled and fitted up as a private residence. The views from the Bay of Ayr are very fine. The river is crossed by two bridges, the Auld and New—" The Twa Brigs " of Burns' poem.

Our driver is a good guide, and points out many places of local and historic interest. The little cottage in which Burns was born on the 25th of January, 1759, is about two miles from Ayr. The original building was a " clay biggin," consisting of two apartments, the kitchen and the "spence" or sitting-room. The house was surrounded by seven acres of ground. It is now the property of the Ayr Burns' Monument Trustees, and is set apart as a museum in which relics of the poet are preserved. Burns' monument stands in the centre of an acre of ground prettily laid out. In an apartment here are exhibited various editions of the poet's works, a copy of the original portrait of Burns, and the Bible given by Burns to Highland Mary when they plighted their troth. From the upper part of the monument is a good view of the surrounding country. The poet's grave is at Dumfries, where he died July 21, 1796. There in the old church-

"The little cottage in which Burns was born"

yard of St. Michael's Church is a mausoleum, beneath whose dome stands a marble group of two figures, representing the genius of Coila finding her favorite son at the plough, and casting over him her mantle of inspiration.

Ayr is full of the atmosphere of Burns, and our driver is a true lover of the Ayrshire ploughman. After we have looked upon the original manuscript of "Tam O'Shanter," and later when we are in the graveyard of Alloway Kirk, where Tam saw the witches, he repeats portions of the poem, acting the most exciting parts with great enthusiasm, as he points out the scene of the events. This unexpected addition to the programme is very entertaining.

"Alloway's auld haunted Kirk" is roofless, but the walls are well preserved, and the bell still hangs in the east end as of old. Here are the Tam o' Shanter Inn, and the Auld Brig o' Doon, and the scenes which inspired the exquisite lines beginning:

"Ye banks and braes o' bonny Doon."

The Doon is indeed a bonny river, whose banks are said to be always "fresh and gay." The scenes of some of the most popular poems of Burns are also to be found on the banks of the Ayr, near Mauchline.

From Ayr we continue our journey to Glasgow, and settle ourselves at St. Enoch's Station Hotel. Glasgow is a great city, representing the commerce and manufactures of Scotland, and commanding an enormous foreign and domestic trade. "The origin and meaning of the name Glasgow has been the subject of much debate. It is a term of Celtic origin and high antiquity, among the numerous and conflicting definitions of which are 'the gray smith,' 'the gray hound,' 'the dark glen,' 'the green wood,' and 'the beloved green spot.' The town has existed from a very remote period, and has played no unimportant part in Scottish history. The city is built over a coal field, whose rich seams of ironstone have contributed much to its rapid industrial growth. The river Clyde has also been a source of much of its prosperity and wealth." In 1763 the illustrious James Watt began that memorable series of experiments which resulted in the successful application of steam as a great motive power; and in 1812 Mr. Henry Bell launched on the Clyde his first steam vessel; the first steamer not only on the Clyde but in Europe. Glasgow is a handsome town, with broad, well-made streets, and the two sides of the river are here joined by many bridges. Buchanan Street is the principal and most central street, and there are two beautiful parks situated on high grounds and commanding fine views of the city.

On Tuesday night we attend the Royal Princess Theatre, and are entertained by a spirited rendering of a play entitled "Rob Roy." This morning it rains, and as we have little hope of going out, letter-writing is the order of the day; but after luncheon the sun comes out, and as there is a prospect of a fine afternoon we engage a hansom and drive along the main thoroughfares, first to the Royal Exchange and municipal buildings, which are handsome edifices, then to the Cathedral. The High Kirk, or old Cathedral of Glasgow, is one of the finest examples of early English undecorated Gothic architecture, and contains specimens of every style practised from the twelfth to the seventeenth century. Behind it the Necropolis rises steeply to the top of the Cathedral, forming a beautiful background to the noble building, for it is covered with picturesque shrubberies and rich monuments. We find the interior of the Cathedral well worth our trouble, when, yielding to the persuasion of our driver, we enter its walls. It contains one hundred and forty-seven pillars and one hundred and fifty-nine windows, many of them of exquisite workmanship. The crypt under the choir is superb, unsurpassed, it is said, by any similar structure in Britain. It is now used only as a place of burial. In the southwest corner is St. Mungo's Well, the spot, according to tradition, where the founder first established his cell and church. Sir Walter

Scott has frequently referred to this cathedral in "Rob Roy," and "Rob Roy's Column" is still pointed out to visitors as the spot near which the outlaw stood when warned of his danger.

West End Park is an exclusive region, enveloped in a fashionable, conventional atmosphere. Here is a handsome memorial fountain, whose surmounting bronze figure is that of the "Lady of the Lake." Here, too, is a very popular institution, the City Industrial Museum, which has acquired a fine collection, embracing natural history, ethnology, and especially the industrial arts. The view from Hill Head is delightful. From this point may be seen the city, and the Clyde with its forest of masts, and immense steamers which travel up and down the river and connect Glasgow with every part of the world. Ben Lomond also towers up in the far distance, and from the very top of the hill one may behold Glasgow University.

The following is an extract from the *North British Daily Mail* of September 12, 1896:

THE RAILWAY RACE IN AMERICA — ALL RECORDS BROKEN.

BUFFALO, Sept. 11th.

A special train on the New York Central Railroad left New York at 5 hours 40 minutes 30 seconds this morning. It arrived at East Buffalo at 12 hours 34 minutes 57 seconds, having thus covered 436½ miles in 6 hours 54 minutes 27 seconds. The actual time of running, exclusive of stoppages to change engines, was 6 hours 47 minutes, and the average speed maintained was 64⅓ miles an hour. The previous English record was 63¼ miles an hour. The weight of the New York Central train was 175 tons, while that of the English train was 106 tons. During almost the entire journey the American train was in the teeth of a heavy wind.—*Reuter*.

To-day we have set for a tour around Loch Lomond, Inversnaid, Stronachlachar, Loch Katrine, the Trossachs, Loch Achray, Aberfoyle, and the circular coaching tour around Loch Ard. It is to be one of the " Banner " days of our Scottish trip, and will include travel by railway, steamer, coach and trap.

We breakfast at seven o'clock, and take the

The Land of Burns, Glasgow, etc.

train at Queen Street Station for Balloch. Here the pretty steam yacht *Queen* is waiting for us, and after an hour's sail on Loch Lomond, will leave us at Inversnaid. This part of the trip is most delightful, in spite of a heavy shower of a half hour. Loch Lomond is one of the loveliest of the Scottish lakes. At the north its gradually narrowing banks vanish among the dusky mountain gorges, while its southern shores spread and open among the bays and headlands of a beautiful, fertile country. Innumerable picturesque islands of every shape and size render the picture one that can hardly be surpassed. Enchanting scenery surrounds it. The mountains towering high on every side, add their sublimity to the view. No pen can describe, no photograph can give even a faint idea of the beauty that lies about us. It is not wonderful that Scott was inspired with all this wealth of material around him.

We land regretfully at last, and at Inversnaid find a large coach and four powerful horses waiting to carry us to Stronachlachar. This is a most enjoyable ride; the air is so pure and invigorating that the forty-five minutes of its duration pass all too quickly. On the way we see the hut of Rob Roy, and the cottage in which his wife was born. This is the country of Rob Roy. Sir Walter Scott has peopled the Trossachs for us, and given to these wild glens and moors a fantastic charm that rivals in interest the bloom of the heather which we see around us for miles on every side. Our driver tells us that grouse abound in this region.

All about us rise the majestic mountains, and our road carries us so high at times that we almost imagine ourselves bounding over their summits. Now we have reached Stronachlachar, at the head of Loch Katrine, where there is a comfortable hotel in which the most persistent appetite of a hungry tourist can be satisfied. An hour later we descend the hill and take the small steamer which can just be seen rounding the bend in the loch. We have many fellow-

"Enchanting scenery surrounds us," Loch Lomond

passengers on this trip; from eighty to a hundred: some Scotch, the greater number English, and a few American tourists. Loch Katrine is a lovely sheet of water lying at the feet of the rugged heights. It has attained a world-wide fame as the scene of Scott's poem, "The Lady of the Lake." But Wordsworth and other poets have also immortalized this enchanting region, and history lurks in every height and depth and secret by-way. All is beautiful beyond description. Numberless mountains, with many peaks and ridges guard the lake. Ben Lomond is the king of these: rising nearly thirty-two hundred feet above us, and clothed in its rich soft hues of green and brown, it holds watch and ward over the sleeping beauty, a type of everlasting love and protection. On our right is Ben Venue, an enormous mass, gracefully robed in heather and ferns, which have an extremely beautiful effect in the sunlight. This mountain is nearly twenty-four hundred feet high; Ben Ledi, nearly twenty-nine hundred feet. The name of this mountain is Gaelic, said to signify "the Hill of God." On our left is Ben A'an, like Ben Venue, excepting in the great conical rocky peak which rises from its summit, and at our feet myriads of sparkling diamonds reflect the sun's rays on the rippling waters of the lake.

"Every rock has its echo, and every grove is vocal with the melodious harmony of birds."

Roderick Dhu's Watch-tower is a rocky hill rising several hundred feet from the margin of the water on the southern side.

Many islands come into view, the most noted of which is Ellen's Isle, a deserted mass of tangled wilderness—

> "So close with copsewood bound
> Nor track nor pathway might declare
> That human foot frequented there;"

but never to be forgotten, for it is "linked with a star," and so destined to immortality.

Our little steamer lands us on the Trossachs Pier, from which point we are to coach through the Trossachs and along charming Loch Achray to Aberfoyle. As we drive along the beautiful macadamized roads, with the dense masses of pine, birch and other foliage on either side, we seem to be hedged in ; when the road will turn, or where is the next point of exit, is quite puzzling. So lovely and primitive is the scene that one might imagine himself wandering in a veritable fairy-land. We come out through the Pass of the Trossachs upon a magnificent view. A picturesque valley extends for miles and miles before us, bordered by lofty mountains. Just now a mist forming on the summits absorbs the sun's rays, producing a most brilliant rainbow. What more could one desire to render the scene perfect? A masterpiece of the Great Artist. Every one is enraptured, and when a fresh view bursts upon us, our driver stops his horses, and inspired by our appreciation, exclaims enthusiastically : " This is our grandest view of all."

Not so, think I, for all are so sublime in individual beauty, it seems impossible to praise one beyond another.

Now, we come to a very steep hill, and the driver putting on the brakes, with a twirl of his long whip, keeps his horses at an even pace. The road seems dangerous. At times one feels that the coach may overturn, but no, the driver knows his business and his horses, and we turn the corners with ease and grace. Our coach is a beauty; of solid oak oiled; four horses, silver mounted harness; and the "Whip," a typical Scotchman, with bright red jacket, and tall white hat; every inch a horseman. We have about twenty-eight passengers. Suddenly the lines are tightened, our "Whip" shouts "whoa," and we are landed safe and sound at the Bailie Nicol Jarvie Hotel at Aberfoyle at 3.15 p. m. Three other coaches arrive about the same time from the Trossachs. While these latter tourists have "done" the Lakes and Trossachs, and will return to Glasgow and Edinburgh by the 3.50 p. m. train from Aberfoyle, we are yet to make a tour of thirteen and a half miles by trap, ere we return to Glasgow.

We order lunch, and engage the trap to be ready at four o'clock. Our driver is on hand at the stroke of the hour, and away we go for a ride around Loch Ard. This is a beautiful sheet of water. The remains of Duchray Castle, a rather uninteresting building, appear on an island on the south side of the loch, and we have several fine views of Ben Lomond. There is also here a water-fall celebrated as the retreat of Flora MacIvor, the heroine of Waverley. Now we are ascending a mountain road, and quite on the summit we see a huge iron pipe projecting from one side. Our driver tells us that this pipe conducts the water of Loch Katrine to the city of Glasgow, and that this is the sole water supply of the city. As Loch Katrine lies at a greater elevation than Glasgow, the water has a natural flow, thus saving the city considerable expense.

After a delightful drive of more than two hours, we alight before the hotel at Aberfoyle, where we are warmed and refreshed by a cup of tea and some hot toast. At nine o'clock we reach the St. Enoch's Station Hotel, Glasgow, thus completing one of the most interesting of our excursions. Scotland may well be proud of her " bonny Highland Country."

The Highlands—
   Staffa and Iona—
      Fingal's Cave—
         Inverness

The Highlands—Staffa and Iona—Fingal's Cave—Inverness.

Greenock—*En route* for Oban—Dunoon—Rothesay—Kyles of Bute—Maids of Bute—Tarbert—Crinan Canal—Oban—Castle Dunstaffnage—Staffa—Fingal's Cave — The Causeway — Bending Pillars—Fingal's Wishing Chair—Iona—The Street of the Dead — The Cemetery — Ballachulish — Glencoe — Ossian's Cave—Scene of the Massacre—Benavie—Ben Nevis—Fort Augustus—Inverness—The Northern Meeting—Scotch Pipers—A noted Character—Away to Edinburgh—Scenes on the Journey—Farewell to the Highlands.

WE leave St. Enoch's Station this morning for Glasgow, arriving at nine o'clock, and immediately taking the steamer *Columba* for Oban. Dunoon, our first stopping place, is a popular resort on the Clyde, with the ruins of the old, and the modern structure of the new castle overlooking the pier. Our passage is rather squallish, and some of the passengers are sick. On the boat we make the acquaintance of a young English couple who are taking our identical trip. We at once establish friendly relations with each other. Our next station is Rothesay, well known in ancient history, with its ruined castle, once a residence of the kings of Scotland. Here is a fine esplanade facing the bay and commanding beautiful views. Now we pass through the famous Kyles of Bute, a picturesque channel between the mouth of the Clyde and Loch Fyne, separating the Island of Bute from the main-land. From the steamer's deck we can see the "Maids of Bute," a couple of queer-looking stones standing close together, and painted to resemble two old maids sitting upon the mountain side.

The Scottish hills are very attractive, and this scenery all along the route is quite different from the English and Irish country. We stop at Tarbert for passengers. This is a fishing village, pleasantly situated, but of no especial importance; still it has its old castle overlooking the harbor, and during the herring-fishing season

The Highlands—Fingal's Cave

an immense number of boats may be seen here, and they have a lively time. At eleven o'clock we reach Ardrishaig, and here bid good-bye to the *Columba*, as she is too large a steamer to cruise up the Crinan Canal. Passengers and freight are transferred to the *Linnet*, a smaller boat. This journey is delightful. The canal is very narrow. It was made about the year 1800 to avoid the circuitous passage of seventy miles around the Mull of Kintyre, and is nine miles long, having fifteen locks, thirteen of which are only ninety-six feet long, twenty-four feet wide and twelve feet deep.

The captain tells us if we wish to walk a mile or two, to go ahead of the steamer and enjoy the country while she is passing through some of the locks. This many of us do, and we have a picturesque walk. We are impressed with the clean appearance of the houses here, as well as the beauty around us.

The islands of Islay, Jura and Scarba are now in view, and the whirlpool of Corrivreckin, caused by the Atlantic tide rushing through the space between Jura and Scarba at eighteen miles an hour. Scarba Mountain is before us, 1470 feet high, and beyond it is the noble Ben More, the highest mountain in Mull, 3179 feet.

The *Linnet* carries us to Crinan, where we change once more to a large steamer, the *Chevalier*, and proceed directly to Oban. The scenery all along the route is superb; huge masses of rock loom up on either side, and the waves dash ceaselessly against them. It is impossible to forget the grandeur of these sights. The approach of evening adds new beauties to the view.

This delightful experience is cut short by our arrival at Oban, which is our destination for the next few days. It is five o'clock when we reach the Station Hotel.

It is a well-known fact that all the station hotels throughout Scotland are under railroad management, and are first-class in every particular. Our experience confirms this statement.

The Highlands—Fingal's Cave

Sunday being clear and pleasant, in company with our English friends, we take a walk of seven miles to Castle Dunstaffnage. This famous ruin, guarding the entrance to Loch Etive, was the seat of Scottish monarchy until the overthrow of the Picts, when Scone succeeded to that honor. A cranny in the castle wall is shown as the original repository of the celebrated Stone of Destiny, or Lia Fail, which forms the support of the coronation chair in Westminster Abbey. It is also called the Dunstaffnage Stone, and the Stone of Scone. I have said before that the ancient Scottish kings were crowned on this stone. It was transferred from Dunstaffnage Castle to the Abbey of Scone, and removed to Westminster by Edward I. in 1296.

The country hereabout is wild and picturesque, affording abundant opportunity for excursions by car and steamer. The most famous as well as most interesting expedition is that to Staffa and Iona. It is one hundred and twenty miles by sea, and occupies a day.

The day fixed for our journey thither proves rainy, but that does not deter us, and at eight o'clock in the morning we find ourselves on the large steamer H. M. S. *Grenadier*, on our way to the noted islands. A rough voyage brings us within sight of Staffa, where we anchor, and are met by a large boat, into which we all, thirty in number, step, and are rowed to the island of the world-renowned Fingal's Cave. We follow our guide over stones shaped much like those at the Giant's Causeway. This is a wonderful spot, almost beyond adequate description. The whole end of the island is supported by natural columns averaging fifty feet in height, and following in their course the indentations of the land. The bases of these colums form the cave, which is lighted from without to its farthest extremity. The upright pillars, which constitute the entrance, are of the most perfect regularity. The waters of the sea are the floor of the cave, and they never ebb entirely out, but beat with violence against the walls, which glisten as if covered

"We are rowed to the island."

The Highlands—Fingal's Cave

with myriads of diamonds. I will never forget this sight, nor the roar of the waves dashing their foam in all directions. I quote the following paragraph from Troil's "Letters on Iceland":

"How splendid do the porticos of the ancients appear in our eyes, and with what admiration are we seized on seeing even the colonnades of our modern edifices. But when we behold the Cave of Fingal, formed by nature, it is no longer possible to make a comparison, and we are forced to acknowledge that this piece of architecture, executed by nature, far surpasses that of the Louvre, that of St. Peter at Rome, and even what remains of Palmyra and Pestum, and all that the genius, the taste and the luxury of the Greeks were ever capable of inventing."

It is not strange that legend should name this cave as the abode of a hero. I cannot refrain from repeating also these lines of Sir Walter Scott:

"The shores of Mull on the eastward lay,
And Ulva dark, and Colonsay,
And all the group of islets gay
　　That guard famed Staffa round.
Then all unknown, its columns rose,
Where dark and undisturbed repose
　　The cormorant had found,
And the shy seal had quiet home,
And weltered in that glorious dome,
Where, as to shame the temples deck'd
By skill of earthly architect,
Nature herself, it seemed would raise
A Minster to her Maker's praise.
Not for a meaner use ascend
Her columns, or her arches bend;
Nor of a theme less solemn tells
That mighty surge that ebbs and swells,
And still between each awful pause,
From the high vault an answer draws,
In varied tones, prolonged and high,
That mocks the organ's melody.
Nor doth its entrance front in vain
To old Iona's holy fane,
That Nature's voice might seem to say,
'Well hast thou done, frail child of clay!
Thy humble powers that stately shrine
Tasked high and hard—but witness mine.'"

"The renowned Fingal's Cave"

From the cave we are led around the Causeway to view the Corner-Stone, the only square stone on the island. Here also we have a fine sight of the Bending Pillars, columns apparently bowed by the mass of rock above them. On the Causeway is Fingal's Wishing Chair with the usual legend attached, save that here the condition is that three distinct wishes shall be made.

From the summit of the island may be seen MacKinnon's, or, as it is called, Cormorant's Cave, also Iona with its Cathedral Tower, and farther off Big Colonsay, Islay and Jura, and to the left the Tresnish Islands, Coll, Tiree and the rest. Looking down over the Causeway, the view is wonderful. Pillars and stones of every shape and position, and of every size, are fitted into each other as if by human hands. Having seen this place and the Giant's Causeway, one can readily credit the supposition that both are parts of the same once continuous immense bed of columnar basalt.

As we leave Staffa, our boat keeps close to

the caves, giving us an opportunity of observing them from the sea.

At three o'clock we reach Iona, and, as at Staffa, the steamer is anchored and passengers taken ashore in a row boat. As a matter of history, I copy here a brief extract relating to this island: "Icolmkill, or I-Columb-kill, was called by monkish writers Iona, I-signifies Island, which was its original name, until St. Columba having founded a monastery there, it came to be called I-Columb-kill, the island of Columba's cell. Its ancient religious edifices were established about the year 565 by St. Columba, who left his home in Ireland to preach Christ to the Picts. The Church is said to have been built by Queen Margaret, towards the end of the eleventh century. It is in the form of a cross. In the middle of this cathedral rises a tower supported by four arches, and ornamented by bass-reliefs. Here are the tombs of forty-eight Scottish kings, four kings of Ireland; eight Norwegian monarchs, and one king of France. The cell of

Columba became the mother of one hundred monasteries, and here the princes and nobles of Scotland were sent to be educated. It was the favorite sepulchre of the Scotch and Irish kings."

The word Iona is said to be derived from a Hebrew word signifying a dove; and the Gaelic Li-hona means the Blessed or Sacred Isle. Tourists are led first to the ruins of the Nunnery by the official guide. This was erected about the close of the twelfth century, and is still comparatively well preserved. The chancel, nave and part of the vaulted roof remain. Within the Church is the tomb of the Prioress Anna, and other defaced monuments. Thence we walk along the "Straid-na-Marbh," or street of the dead, to the burial ground of Iona, called Reilig Oran. Maclean's Cross, which we pass on the way, is one of those Runic crosses for which the island is famous; it is noticeable for its beautiful scroll carving, and is said to be the oldest cross in Scotland.

In the cemetery we see groups of ancient tombstones, most of them carved in relief, and possessing great antiquarian and historical interest. The finest tomb in the burial ground is the memorial slab of the Four Friars. The most ancient structure on the island is St. Oran's Chapel, supposed to have been erected about the close of the eleventh century by Margaret, Queen of Malcolm Canmore, on the site of St. Columba's original cell. Opposite the west door of the Cathedral is the noble monument, known as the Iona Cross, erected to the memory of St. Martin of Tours, who lived in the sixth century. In the Cathedral are innumerable effigies cut in the walls and the stones of the pavement, and inscriptions in ancient characters and in the Latin tongue nearly obliterated by time. In the centre of the chancel is the largest tombstone in Iona, that of Macleod of Macleod. Beside the royal tombs here are also the sepulchres of many Lords of the Isles, bishops, abbots, and priors, as well as Chiefs of the MacKinnons, Macleans, MacQuar-

"WE WALK ALONG THE 'STREET OF THE DEAD'"

The Highlands—Fingals' Cave

ries and other clans. The Duke of Argyll has had some excavations made, displaying the original foundations and plans of the ancient structures, and uncovering many splendidly carved stones, which have lain for centuries beneath masses of rubbish.

"Lone Isle, though storms have round thy turrets rode,
  Thou wert the temple of the living God,
  And taught earth's millions at His shrine to bow,
  Though desolation wraps thy glories now.
  Still thou wilt be a marvel through all time
  For what thou hast been, and the dead who rest
  Around the fragments of thy walls sublime
  Once taught the world and harbored many a guest,
  And ruled the warriors of each northern clime;
  Thou'rt in the world like some benighted one,
  Home of the mighty that have passed away.
  Hail! Sainted Isle! Thou art a holy spot
  Engraved on many hearts; and thou art worth
  A pilgrimage, for glories long gone by,
  Thou noblest College of all the ancient earth.
  Virtue and Truth, Religion itself shall die
  Ere thou canst perish from the chart of fame,
  Or darkness shroud the halo of thy name."

The town of Iona maintains a large fishing interest, but can boast of very few modern residences. There is much beauty in the rocks and the sandy beach along the shores of the island. Our guide is very solemn as he escorts us from place to place, and relates events and historic details; and we too, as we realize the meaning of these ancient monuments, are more and more impressed with the wonderful influence once possessed by this little island when made the source from which the light of Christianity spread itself over the northwestern Caledonian regions. We feel that we are on hallowed ground: the consecration of the past lingers in its atmosphere, and we are reluctant to leave its awe-inspiring associations.

Six o'clock finds us in Oban again, after ten hours spent in visiting the world-renowned islands.

To-day, notwithstanding the pouring rain, we wend our way to the pier where the steamer *Mountaineer* awaits passengers for Ballachulish.

The Highlands—Fingal's Cave

This trip is not very interesting, as we steam up Loch Linnhe through mist and rain. At the Ballachulish Hotel we have luncheon and engage a carriage to take us to Glencoe.

Passing through the village, which is inhabited by the workmen of the neighboring slate quarries, and is a pretty little place, we drive along the bank of Loch Leven, surrounded by lofty mountain scenery, which has been the inspiration of many poets and authors, and enter the Pass of Glencoe at the bridge where the road skirts the River Coe, between the great Sgor-na-Ciche, 2430 feet high, and Meall Mor, 2215 feet. The spot is wild and desolate, with a dreary yet sublime magnificence. The peculiar character of this glen is the absence of trees. The peaks look like enormous cones, with great channels made in their steep rugged sides by the water courses. The vegetation is sparse, and there are no cattle here, or other signs of life. As we ride onward, we are ever surrounded by these groups of tall stern mountains, in close proximity to each other. Prominent among them is the majestic Bidean-nam-Bian. Here is Signal Rock, and a beautiful water-fall descending from a lofty summit is pointed out as "Ossian's Shower Bath," while almost on the mountain top is visible the hollow known as Ossian's Cave. Only one person, it is said, has attempted the ascent to this cave; an old shepherd who declared afterwards that he would never repeat the perilous expedition. The cave is at an elevation of about two thousand feet. We have reached the scene of the massacre. The carriage halts and we look upon the spot where a dastardly deed of vengeance was accomplished, which has left an indelible blot on the annals of the English nation. The Clan MacDonald were here massacred by the English in 1692. The story runs somewhat as follows: "A proclamation had been issued, offering indemnity to such insurgents as should take the oath of allegiance to King William III., on or before the last day of December. But while most of the chiefs who

"WE HAVE REACHED THE SCENE OF THE MASSACRE".

had been in arms for James soon took advantage of the proclamation, MacDonald, of Glencoe, was prevented by accident rather than design from tendering his submission within the time. The king, persuaded that the MacDonalds were the main obstacles to the pacification of the Highlands, sanctioned the sanguinary orders for proceeding to military execution against the clan, and the secretary urged the officers in command to use the utmost rigor. Campbell, of Glenlyon, accordingly repaired to Glencoe on the first of February with a hundred and twenty men. Being uncle to young MacDonald's wife, he was received by the chief with the utmost friendship and hospitality, and the men were lodged with free quarters in the houses of the clan. Till the 13th of the month the troops lived in harmony and familiarity with the people, and on the very night of the massacre, Glenlyon passed the evening at cards in his own quarters with Mac-Donald's sons. In the night Lieutenant Lindsay, with a party of soldiers, called in a friendly manner at the chieftain's house, and was instantly admitted. MacDonald, while in the act of dressing himself and giving orders for refreshments for his guests, was shot dead at his own bedside. The slaughter became general, and neither age nor sex was spared. Several who fled to the mountains perished by famine and the inclemency of the season."

This weird spot is peopled only by the ghosts of the dead. Nothing seems to thrive here, and we are glad to move on to more cheerful scenes.

We leave Ballachulish, as we entered it, in a pouring rain. We take the steamer *Fusilier* on the Caledonian Canal as far as Fort William, proceed by rail to Banavie, then change again to a small steamboat, the *Glencarry*. These boats are all side-wheelers. Here we have a fine view of Ben Nevis looking every inch of its 4400 feet. The magnificent panorama here is indescribable and never to be forgotten : the scenery is wild and picturesque in the extreme. Now our passage is along the River Lochy as far as the lake

"WE HAVE A FINE VIEW OF BEN NEVIS."

The Highlands—Fingal's Cave

of the same name. This is a beautiful body of water, on either side of us are still the mountains, covered with forests, while here and there may be seen the crops of the thrifty farmer.

Now we are on Loch Oich, the centre of this great chain, as well as the most elevated of these lakes, "the Summit Level of the Canal." It is about four miles in length and a quarter of a mile wide, and several pretty green islands adorn its bosom. From the loch to the River Oich, and on till we arrive at Fort Augustus are four consecutive locks, through which our little steamer must pass. This occupies an hour: we all go ashore during the process, and make purchases of candy, milk and other refreshments.

Fort Augustus is a pretty village, deriving its name from the military fort built in 1729 to intimidate the Highland clans. There is but little of the old fort left to-day, and on its foundations now stands St. Benedict's Abbey and School, a most imposing monastic institution. The village is situated at the southwestern extremity of Loch Ness, and we have a long, delightful ride on this lake, with a fine view of the famous cataract of Foyers. These falls, for there are two falls, about a quarter of a mile apart, are called the " Fall of Smoke," in consequence of the misty vapor which they send up. The lower fall descends in a sheet of dazzling spray of snowy whiteness into a deep basin surrounded by huge towering rocks. The upper fall is broken in its descent, and an arched bridge spans the chasm. How we enjoy the pure air and beautiful scenery of this western Highland country. The afternoon has cleared up, and the sun shines on the mountain tops.

We pass many typical Scotch scenes, and at last arrive at Inverness, and the Palace Hotel there. We feel that fortune favors us when we learn that the autumn meeting of the Highland games is to be held here to-day and to-morrow. This occasion is known as " The Northern Meeting." What luck!

Various clubs and ladies and gentlemen from

"We have a long and delightful ride on Loch Ness."

all parts of the country come to witness these games, and well they may, for the finest talent and skill in this line of exercise are here brought into competition.

We enter the grounds at one o'clock, and find about five thousand people assembled, among them, doubtless many of the nobility, besides other celebrities. The games last from one o'clock until six, and prove very entertaining. Our hotel gives a grand dinner in honor of the many society leaders who are here. A fashionable ball is also given in the evening; tickets, one guinea for gentlemen, two guineas for ladies. We do not join this part of the entertainment. I copy here an extract from the *Edinburgh Scotsman*, describing these events:

"The leading event in the Highland season began at Inverness yesterday. Competitions in piping, dancing, and in athletics generally, with a couple of cycle races thrown in as a concession to the spirit of the times, were held in the Northern Meeting Park, and were patronized by an enormous crowd of people. The weather was favorable, although somewhat chilly for the time of year. In the afternoon the sun came out with welcome brightness, and a large crowd of fashionable people followed its example.

"The competition in Pibroch playing occupied several hours, no fewer than seventeen pipers taking part in it. Their playing was, on the whole, not so good as has been heard at the meeting in former years, and as only a few of the competitors showed outstanding merit, the judges had little difficulty in distributing the awards. The coveted gold medal was won by Murdo Mackenzie, piper to Mr. Butter of Faskally, who played The Battle of Waternish. Alexander Mackenzie, Resolis, the second prizeman, played 'I got a Kiss from the King's Hand.'

"The dancing was better than the piping, and needless to say was more appreciated by the majority of the people present.

"John M'Neil, Edinburgh, had the first prize for the fling, and Pipe Major Sutherland, Inver-

"A PRIZE DANCE"

gordon, had the first for the sword dance, the competition being confined to the Northern counties. With hardly an exception the athletic events were confined to competitors resident in the North, and the result was that some of them were not quite so interesting as they would have been, if open to all comers. No records were broken, although contests were keenly entered into.

"The ball last night was a brilliant affair, and was exceedingly enjoyable, the pipers who had won prizes at the games, playing for the Highland dances."

One can hardly imagine what a band of twenty pipers is until he hears them playing together. When accustomed to their peculiar music, it sounds sweet and harmonious.

Inverness, the "capital of the Highlands," is situated, as its name implies, at the mouth of the river Ness, and is surrounded by broad fertile fields, villas and country seats. It has a population of about twenty thousand. We wander about the city, which is a rather quiet place, and visit the stores in which are displayed shawls, scarfs, handkerchiefs, coats and dress stuffs of the various clans; also cairngorms, set in silver or gold, and curiosities peculiar to this region.

Everywhere we see the old Scotch names— Macdonald, Macgregor, Fraser, Bruce, Maclaughlan, Macleod, Campbell and so on.

To the east of the town, on the shores of Murray Frith, is the famous field of Culloden, the scene of the last great battle, and the downfall of the Stuarts. This battle ended also the reign of the Highland chieftains, and the days of their glory, as they had taken sides with the Stuart prince.

While we are in one of the shops, a beautiful collie dog runs up to us and whines until we are compelled to notice him. He rubs himself against us and looks imploringly in our faces. We ask the proprietor of the store whose dog he is, and what he wants, and learn that the fine creature belongs to a jeweller in the neighbor-

"A TYPICAL HIGHLAND WASHDAY"

hood, and that he is able to distinguish strangers visiting the city, and will go up to them and beg till they toss him a penny, sometimes two or three. He has been known to carry a half a dozen pennies in his mouth at once. If one follows him, as we do after giving him a couple of pennies, the dog will be seen to walk slowly to a baker shop close by, enter, and putting his paws on the counter, deposit there the money, and wait till the girl in the shop puts his rolls in a bag, which he carries to a convenient spot on the sidewalk, and there enjoys his luncheon. We are told that he is a well-known character in the town.

In our walks or drives in the suburbs, we occasionally come across a picture in real life like the one on the opposite page, and sometimes it is a very pretty sight to behold a bright, healthy young Scotch lassie singing as she works away with her feet on the family wash. We are much interested whenever we have an opportunity to observe a typical Highland washing-day scene.

In the country especially the washing is performed in this manner, and I can vouch for the satisfactory results of Scotch methods, for it is rare to find people more cleanly in person or clothing than those of the Scotch nation. Accompanied by our friends, we leave Inverness for Edinburgh, taking for our route the Highland Railway, via Forth Bridge, passing through Glen Garry, the Queen's View, Killiecrankie Pass, and over the celebrated bridge which spans the Firth of Forth.

The scenery from Inverness to Edinburgh will always be a pleasant memory to us. It is particularly fine around Glen Garry and the Killiecrankie Pass. The old castle, the lofty mountains, Glengarry forest, the lochs—ravishing pictures are with us on every side for miles and miles. At Killiecrankie Pass, for nearly a mile the banks rise steeply on both sides, and the river is almost hidden in the deep chasm below, as it works its way between the rocks in the dense shadow cast by the overhanging trees or frown-

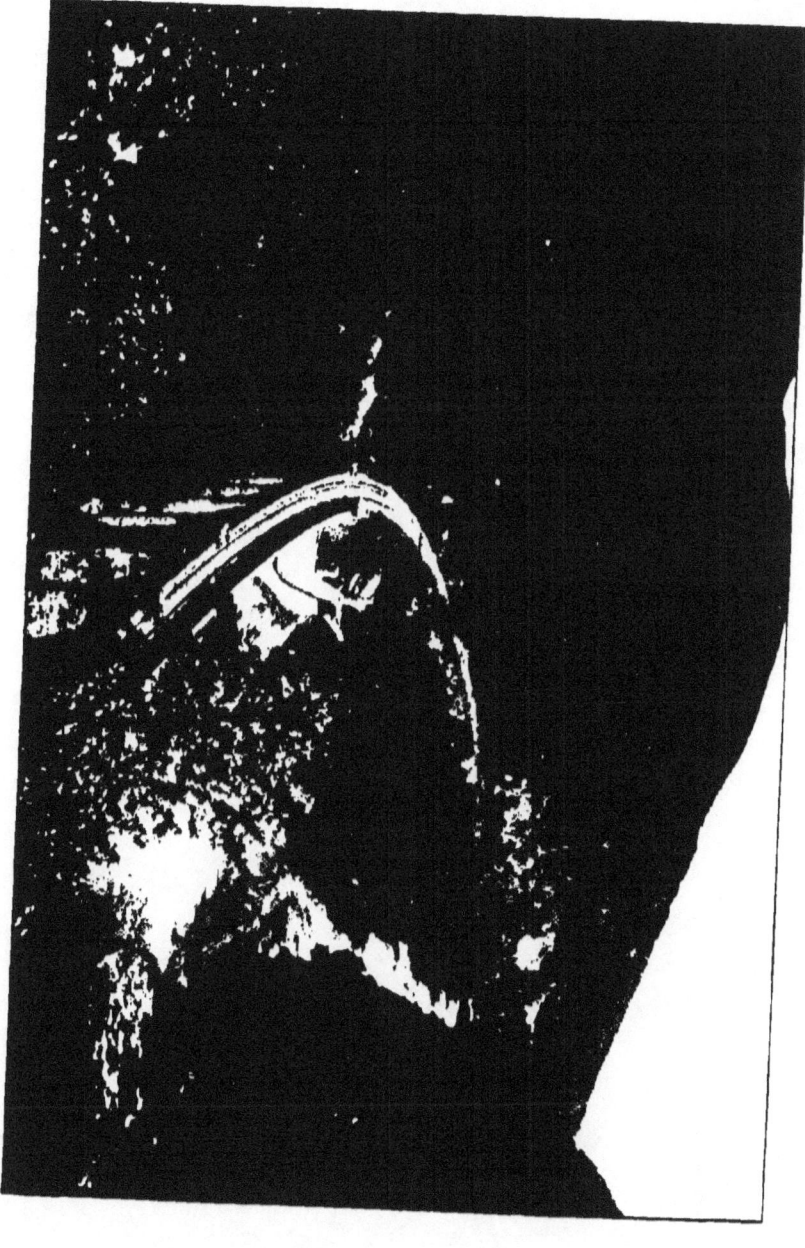

"Queen's View, Killiecrankie Pass"

ing precipices. The right bank, rising like a wall from this dusky depth, is covered with trees to its very summit, blending in a harmonious whole the varying shades of the oak and alder, hazel, birch and fir. The journey of seven and a half hours seems much shorter in the presence of this magnificent panorama. The words of the Rev. Mr. Small so well express the feelings with which these scenes inspire us that I can do no better than repeat them here:

"In rugged grandeur, by the placid lake,
Rise the bold mountain cliffs, sublimely rude,
A pleasing contrast, each with each, they make;
And when in such harmonious union viewed,
Each with more powerful charms appears imbued,
Even thus it is, methinks, with mingling hearts,
Though different far in nature and in mood;
A blessed influence each to each imparts,
Which softens and subdues, yet weakens not, nor
    thwarts."

Edinburgh and the English Lakes—The Home Voyage

Edinburgh and the English Lakes—The Home Voyage

Edinburgh—The Castle—Princes Street—Scott's Monument—St. Giles's Cathedral—Canongate Tolbooth—John Knox's House—White Horse Close—Holyrood—Queen Mary's Apartments—The Queensferry Road—Dean Bridge—Forth Bridge—Farewell to Scotland—Keswick—Lake Derwentwater—Pencil Manufacturers—Greta Hall—The Islands—Drive Around the Lake—By Coach to Windermere—Homes of Shelley and Hall Caine—Wythburn Church—Lake Thirlmere—Helm Crag—Grasmere—Nab Cottage—Rydal Mount—Ambleside—Windermere—Liverpool—The Day of Departure—On Board the *Etruria*—The Voyage—New York—Home Again.

OUR first visit in Edinburgh is to the Castle. This is a noble structure, standing three hundred feet above the valley, upon a cliff which commands a full view of the city. Many associations cluster around these heights. For hundreds of years the Castle was a military stronghold, resisting siege after siege.

Cromwell tried to take it, but its rocky battlements proved inaccessible even to his Ironsides. Crossing a drawbridge, we pass through the old Portcullis Gate, above which may be seen the window of the cell in which the Marquis and Earl of Argyll were confined previous to their execution. Here is the armor room, in which receptions are held, and here in this little room, hardly larger than a closet, Mary, Queen of Scots, gave birth to the prince who was to unite the crowns of England and Scotland. This prince, when eight days old, was let down from the cliff in a basket, that the life so precious to two kingdoms might not perish by murderous hands. Queen Margaret's Chapel is very small, but it is an interesting relic of Norman architecture, named for the Saxon princess, queen of Malcolm Canmore, who died in 1093. On the Bomb Battery, from which one of the finest views of Edinburgh may be seen, is the famous old gun "Mons Meg," supposed to have been made at Mons, in Belgium, in 1486, and celebrated in the history of the Scottish Jameses. It was removed to the Tower of London in 1684, but restored to the Castle in 1829, by the Duke of Wellington, on petition of Sir Walter Scott. The Castle has been the scene of daring exploits. During the conflict between Bruce and Baliol it was taken by the English and held by them for thirty years. In the regalia room are exhibited the crown of Robert Bruce, the sword of state and the jewels of the throne of Scotland, set with gems, and of great value. When Scotland was united with England, in the early part of the eighteenth century, the Scots were afraid these relics would be carried off to to London. They enclosed them in a chest, and closed up the doors and stairways leading to the apartment. They remained there for over a hundred years, until Scott, in delving among the musty records of the city, in search of material for his novels, came across the papers relating to their hiding-place. Every one had forgotten them, but Scott obtained a royal search-warrant, and finally these priceless gems were opened to public view. The Castle, which has served both as a prison and a residence of the Scottish kings, is now used as a barrack, and the gorgeous costumes of the bonny soldier boys make the scene a pleasant one to look upon. Our guide talks much as a parrot, and we grant him only partial attention, as our eyes rove from one point to another of this spot so full of history.

Edinburgh is one of the most picturesque cities in Europe. It is cut in two by a deep gorge, on either side of which the old and the new towns stand facing each other. From our quarters in the Royal Hotel in Princes Street, not far from the beautiful monument to Sir Walter Scott, we can see beyond the ravine the long rows of houses in the old town, and up to the ancient castle, with its immortal associations with Auld Reekie, as the old Scotch people used to call the place.

Scott's monument stands in the eastern

garden. A stair of 287 steps leads to the top, from which there is a fine view. The principal niches are occupied by representations of some of the characters in the Waverley novels. In and around the town we observe hundreds of memorials of this author and his characters.

The architect of the monument, George Keep, a youth of great promise, was drowned before its completion. Scott was born in Edinburgh, and died at Abbotsford, September, 1832, at the age of sixty-one. A fine marble statue of the poet stands at the base of the monument, and is somewhat larger than life.

St. Giles' Cathedral is the ancient parish church of Edinburgh, but it has undergone so many repairs that it presents a rather modern appearance. Here John Knox thundered, and here James VI., the infant who was born in the castle, when chosen to be James I. of England, took leave of his Scottish subjects.

Opposite the northwest corner of St. Giles formerly stood the old Tolbooth Gaol, immortalized by Scott in the " Heart of Midlothian." The site is indicated by the figure of a heart upon the pavement. Canongate Tolbooth, or court-house, was erected in the reign of James VI., and is a good specimen of the architecture of the old town.

We have reached John Knox's house. This manse was provided for the great reformer in 1559, when he was elected minister of Edinburgh, and here he resided until his death in 1572. Over the door is the following inscription:

" Lufe. God. above. all. and. your. neighbor. as. yourself.", and beneath the window from which he is said to have preached to the people, there is a rude effigy of the reformer pointing to the name of God carved upon the stone above in Greek, Latin and English characters. The pulpit from which he preached in St. Giles' Church is now in the Antiquarian Museum.

White Horse Close leads to White Horse Inn, a very old-fashioned building, one of the oldest, and in by-gone days most famous hostelries in the city. It was here Dr. Johnson put up on his arrival in Edinburgh in 1773. Nearly every house in this part of the town is historically famous, and these curious alleys running out of the streets here are all known as "closes."

With feelings of awe we approach the world-renowned Holyrood Palace and Abbey. This ancient pile looms up in solemn grandeur, even now defying time and the elements. The venerable seat of Scottish royalty was originally a convent, as its ordinary name, the Abbey, implies, and like many other monastic institutions, calls David its founder. The legend connected with it is still preserved in the armorial bearings of the borough of the Canongate. The king, so runs the story, was hunting one day in the forest of Drumsheugh, about the year 1128, when he was thrown to the ground and attacked by a stag which had been brought to bay. A cross was suddenly interposed between the defenceless monarch and the furious animal, which fled in dismay at the sight. The cross, the substance of which could not be ascertained, was regarded with the highest veneration. In gratitude for his escape, the king founded and endowed the Church of the Holy Rood.

Here is the Chapel Royal, a fragment of the ancient Abbey, founded by David I. in 1128. This ruin seems frail indeed, and looks as if the present century would have a perceptible effect upon the pillars that still stand. We observe many interesting tombs and monuments, but the chief interest of the palace is associated with the mother of James, the beautiful and ill-fated Mary, Queen of Scots. We recall her sad history as we stand upon the spot where she was married, and walk through the rooms in which she lived. Passing through the audience chamber, where stands the bed on which "Prince Charlie" slept in 1745, we enter Queen Mary's bedroom, which still contains the ancient bed and other furniture. The ceiling here, as in the other rooms, is divided into panels, on which are painted monograms, coats-of-arms and other decorations. On one side is the door of the secret passage by which the conspirators against the life of Rizzio entered, and adjoining is the little supper room where they surprised their victim and dragged him outside the door of the audience chamber, murdering him at the head of the staircase. The stains upon the floor here are said to be blood-stains.

We are quite fatigued by our sight-seeing in Edinburgh. There are so many places that we must visit in this wonderful old town. Arthur's Seat is an abrupt peak, over eight hundred feet high, which terminates the rugged Salisbury Craigs. Across the ravine are other hills, from three to four hundred feet high, and it is on these hills, and in the valleys between that Edinburgh is built, with the many opportunities for handsome structures thoroughly availed of. The city is a succession of statues, memorials, churches, castles and historical sites. No one who has accomplished anything of note is not commemorated in some public way in this most appreciative community. "Edinburgh is handing down to posterity in 'storied urn and animated bust' the memories of all her great people."

Our English friends, who have been our constant companions for the past eight days, bid us good-bye this evening, as they leave Edinburgh for their home at St. Leonards-on-Sea. We shall miss them sadly.

To-day we have planned to see the great Forth Bridge, built for the North British Railway across the Firth of Forth, at Queensferry, nine miles from Edinburgh. It is Sunday, and we learn that the people of this city are very strict in their ideas of keeping the Sabbath. All railway travel, as well as 'buses and trams, is prohibited on that day. In the case of the first and last of these it is an established law, but the 'bus or char-à-banc has protested, and as the proceedings are still in court, it continues to run, in spite of the officials.

At two o'clock this afternoon we secure seats in the open coach, near the driver, and start out with some fourteen other Sabbath-breaking passengers, mostly from our hotel. The driver is a garrulous man, possibly the extra shilling has loosened his tongue, and gives us much information by the way, interspersed with anecdotes and jokes.

This pike, or to speak accurately, the Queensferry Road, runs from London to Inverness. It is a magnificent road. We pass many places of interest—colleges, hotels, asylums, hospitals, residences and noted institutions. Meanwhile the stream of talk flows on. In connection with Sabbath rides, our driver relates that one Sunday as he was starting out, a woman of the Salvation Army thus accosted one of his passengers: "Do you know that you are going to h—— and d——n?" "No," replied the passenger, "I am going to the Forth Bridge." Such is the feeling against Sunday excursions.

We are having a delightful ride. Over Dean Bridge, which spans the water of Leith at a height of 106 feet, we pass, with a fine view on either side, looking downward from the bridge.

Here is one of the stories with which our old "whip" enlivens the way: " Not many miles from here a landlord one day passing the home of one of his tenants perceived John eating his porridge out in the garden in the pouring rain. 'Why, John,' he exclaimed, 'what are you doing out here? Why do you not stay in the house, where it is warm and dry?' 'Ah, mister, my chimney reeks.' 'Well,' said the landlord, 'I will have it fixed at once,' and he advanced towards the house to look into the state of affairs. 'Oh, mister, you must not look at it now,' said John anxiously. 'Yes, but I must and will,' returned the owner, and, suiting the action to the word, he opened the door, and met with a warm reception from John's wife, who rushed at him and beat him over the head with a broom. Fleeing from the spot the landlord was heard to say: 'Ah, John, my good man, sometimes my chimney reeks, too.' "

As we approach the estates of the Earl of Rosebery, which extend miles on either side, our

"The famous bridge which spans the Forth"

talkative Jehu tells us how Lord Rosebery, while at college, made a bet that he would win the Derby and become Prime Minister of England. "And," he adds, "he has done even better, for he has won the Derby twice, and has married a daughter of the Rothschilds."

One anecdote follows another, until we reach the famous bridge which spans the Forth. Here we leave the coach and take a small steamer, which, for sixpence each, carries us under and to the side of this wonderful structure, a marvel even in this nineteenth century of miracles. The guide book states that:

"This magnificent structure was opened for traffic by the Prince of Wales, on the 4th of March, 1890. It was designed by Sir John Fowler and Sir Benjamin Baker, on the ancient and simple principle of the cantilever or balancing brackets, which combines the support of an arch with the tension of a suspension bridge. It was in process of construction seven years, under the superintendence of these gentlemen and Sir

William Arrol, the contractor, who displayed wonderful ingenuity, energy and resource in overcoming the stupendous physical difficulties of so gigantic a work. It consists of two huge steel girders, bridges of 1710 feet span, besides smaller ones on either side, equal to the enormous pressure of 112 pounds to the square foot. Several of the principal piers or foundations of these great spans were built up from the bottom of the sea with great 'caissons,' or metal cases gradually filled with concrete and sand. The northern central pier rests partly on Inchgarvie Island. From the base of the deepest pier to the top of the cantilevers is 450 feet, and the clear space under the centre spans above the surface of the water is 150 feet. It is thus the loftiest bridge in the world, and its total length is 1 mile and 1000 yards. Over 50,000 tons of steel were used in its structure, and it cost over 3,000,000 pounds. It was built to shorten the distance between Edinburgh and Perth."

To-day we bid farewell to dear Scotland.

How reluctant we are to leave her beautiful lakes and mountains! What pleasure we have had in the countless picturesque views which have been ever before us in these past weeks! Memory takes us back to Oban, Iona, Staffa, the Valley of Glencoe, and all the fair Scottish lochs, Lomond, Katrine and Ard; and to Scott's romantic Trossachs, and the noble mountains, and to the noblest of all, lofty Ben Nevis; and the delightful sail on the Caledonian Canal to Inverness; and beautiful Edinburgh with its interesting walks and drives, its monuments and memorials. How happy these days have been! Long, long will they linger in our hearts. As the train pulls out of Waverly Station, we murmur softly and regretfully: "Good-bye, dear Scottish land, good-bye."

"Farewell to the Highlands, farewell to the North;
The birthplace of Valor, the country of Worth;
Wherever I wander, wherever I rove,
The hills of the Highlands forever I love.

"Farewell to the mountains, high covered with snow;
Farewell to the straths and green valleys below;
Farewell to the forests and wild hanging woods,
Farewell to the torrents and loud pouring floods."

We make several changes between Edinburgh and Keswick, stopping on the way at Melrose Station, where we have a fine view of the Abbey from the car window. The Abbey of St. Mary at Melrose was founded by David I. in 1126. Among the other religious edifices on the Scottish border, it suffered from many acts of violence, but it is beautiful even in its ruins, and its graceful and luxuriant style places it in the highest rank of ecclesiastical architecture. Here, it is said, rest the remains of Alexander II., and here was deposited the heart of King Robert the Bruce. Keswick is a pretty little town of about 4000 inhabitants, where we observe some very attractive shops.

We stroll to Lake Derwentwater. This is one of the most beautiful of the English lakes.

"We stroll to Lake Derwentwater".

It is about three miles long, and one mile wide, and is surrounded by steep wooded crags and lovely green hills, with charming little islands resting upon its surface. We are delighted with this spot, and engaging one of the many small boats that are to be seen at the water's edge, I take off coat and vest, and we make the tour of the lake. The water is smooth, and the day is cloudless. As we row along, we pass a picturesque point clad in a robe of green, purple and other softened hues, and known as Friar's Crag. Numerous mountains seem to close the prospect ahead of us. Three hours pass rapidly by as we loiter on this bewitching lake, and we get up good appetites for luncheon.

This afternoon we visit the pencil factory of Banks & Co., and find much to interest us within the walls of this old building. Here are the grinding and pressing rooms, the sawing department, painting and polishing rooms, and packing office. In the latter, a middle-aged woman is seated at a long table tying pencils in packages of a dozen each. She does not count the pencils as she takes them up, yet every time only twelve pencils are removed from the pile. I ask if she never makes a mistake, and am told that for every package found to contain more or less than twelve pencils, I may have a present of a pound in gold. She works with almost incredible rapidity. In the sample room we purchase pencils, seven, twelve, eighteen, twenty-four, and even thirty inches long. The last may also be used as walking sticks. We are presented with a box, showing the entire process, from the rock lead to the finished pencil. I see in imagination, at this moment, an artist out sketching with one of these pencils, thirty inches long. It hardly belongs to the vest pocket series.

Not far from the old mill is Greta Hall, the residence of the poet Southey, from 1803 until his death in 1843. A monument to the poet may be seen in the little Crosthwaite Church, beyond the bridge which crosses the Greta. Shelley also lived for a time in this locality.

There are many interesting associations connected with Lake Derwentwater and its islands, three of which may be seen from the shore. These are Derwent Isle, Lord's Island, and beyond the latter, Herbert Island. All three are the subject of legend and tradition. Herbert Island was the abode of the saint whose name it bears, and the remains of his cell in the middle of the island bear witness to this fact. St. Herbert lived in the seventh century.

A thousand years later, we hear of Lady Derwentwater issuing from the family mansion on Lord's Isle, and flying up Wallow Crag, this wooded height on the side of the lake, and by the Lady's Rake, on her way to London, in a desperate effort to save the life of her rebel lord, who perished on the scaffold for participating in the rebellion of 1715.

To-day we drive around the beautiful lake. The sky is clear and as blue as cobalt; not a cloud is visible, and the air is delightful. We behold a series of varied and charming views.

Here is a lovely little wooded height called Castle Head, and farther on are the Barrow Falls, which, however, cannot bear comparison with the Lodore Falls, but a short distance beyond. We pass through a little village, and ascend a ridge which affords us a good view of the surrounding country. Here is Cat Bells' Ridge, and here a woods on the side of the road, and onward we go till we reach our hotel again. Afar, the mountains tower in varied hues of purple, green and umber, while along the slopes flocks of sheep and other cattle graze quietly upon the abundant grass and heather.

The rumble of wheels and the clatter of horses' feet announce the tally-ho that is to carry us to Windermere, the largest of the English lakes. We are fortunate in having already engaged the box seats, for an excursion party goes by this coach to Ambleside. The party numbers twenty-nine, including the " Whip " and eight musicians, who are good enough to enliven the ride with a variety of choice (?) music.

An elderly English lady sitting back of us seems quite irritated by the music. She leans over, and in tones by no means modulated, declares it to be " beastly, and at times, horrid."

The weather is fine and our horses travel well over these steep mountain roads. Now and then the men jump off, while one of the ladies takes the reins and drives skilfully to the mountain top. Looking back, we have a magnificent view of Lake Derwentwater and Bassenthwaite. Here the road is seven hundred feet above the level of the sea.

Our driver points out the home of Shelley, and the residences of Hall Caine and the Bishop of Bath, pretty and attractive, but unpretentious spots. We have now in full view, a large mountain, which resembles an enormous elephant; head, ears, eyes and long trunk are faithfully represented. When nothing of especial interest presents itself, the band favors us with national airs, much to the annoyance of the English lady, who, by the way, complains much of everything.

The wonder is that she allows herself to take the trip at all.

"Whoa," shouts the driver, and we stop before Wythburn Church and Inn. We do not enter the Inn, but *in* we must go to the little old church, a quaint and cosy place, capable of accommodating a hundred and fifty worshippers. After fifteen minutes spent in resting and looking about us, we are again on the way. Here is a fine view of Lake Thirlmere, and farther on, of Helm Crag. The lake is three miles long, and scarcely a third of a mile wide; near the middle it narrows to a few yards in width, and is spanned by a small wooden bridge. This is a beautiful picture, with Helvellyn to the left, and Skiddaw in the distance. Helm Crag is noted for the peculiar formation of the rocks on its crest, which are a fair representation of the oft-quoted passage of Scripture: "The lion and the lamb shall lie down together."

The placid and picturesque waters of Grasmere Lake are about a mile long and nearly a half a mile wide. A solitary green island gleams like an emerald upon its surface. We stop at an old hotel in the neighborhood for rest and luncheon. The village, a simple, unpretending place, has been celebrated by the poetry of Wordsworth. We peep into the church, and stroll through the church-yard, in which are the graves of Coleridge and Wordsworth.

Refreshed by the luncheon and short rest, the band plays more sweet melodies, and off we whirl, leaving behind us the town of Grasmere and some five and twenty villagers who have come out of their houses on the roadside, attracted by the music.

This neat little stone building is Nab Cottage, once the home of the poet Hartley Coleridge, and here is the far-famed Rydal Mount, the home of Wordsworth during the latter years of his life; and close by is the village of Rydal. We are on a pretty road, with fields on either side. Our driver, always faithful to his duty, points out the spot where Wordsworth was wont to sit. The poet's favorite haunt is a pile of rocks of various shapes, well shaded by oaks and chestnut trees, with some shrubbery, not far from the quiet waters of Rydal.

As we look backwards towards Rydal Hall and the village in the distance, we gaze upon a lovely picture. The poet's house, on a hill behind the church, is almost hidden by trees. Within the grounds of Rydal Hall the charming little Falls of the Rydal send forth a musical voice, and the wooded mountains stand calm and beautiful in their green foliage. The scene vanishes, our well-tried steeds keep up their steady pace, and the only sounds now heard are the rumble of the coach and the occasional cracking of the whip, save when the band breaks forth in sudden melody, or the discontented English passenger utters her complaints. In silence we feast our eyes upon the romantic scenes around us.

At Ambleside we take another coach, and bid farewell to the English lady and her companions. Ambleside is beautifully situated in the valley of

the Rothay. It is supposed to have been a Roman station, as fragments of tesselated pavements and other relics have been found in the neighborhood. It is a head-quarters for excursions in the southern part of the Lake District. With a lingering backward glance at the picturesque spot, we start onward, and reach Oiggs' Hotel at Windermere without incident, at three o'clock in the afternoon.

This morning we take a drive which embraces a general outline of the attractions of this celebrated place. We ride ten or twelve miles along the most frequented, as well as most secluded roads. Yesterday's journey also helps to fill out our view of the northern, middle and southern portions of Lake Windermere. It is the largest lake in England, being ten miles and a half long, and a third of a mile wide. It has many landings, and these with the numberless sail boats upon the water, its beautiful wooded banks, varied by picturesque villas and the lofty mountains to be seen on either side, render this one of the most delightful regions in the country. The celebrated region known as the Lake District embraces a wealth of diversified scenery, with mountains and lakes, which, though not excelling by their great size, present a more wildly picturesque panorama than one would expect who has not seen them. There are in all about sixteen lakes or meres, besides innumerable mountain tarns. The highest mountains are Scafell Pike, Scafell, Helvellyn and Skiddaw, and these range from three thousand to three thousand two hundred feet in height. The Lake School of Poetry has made the district its own, and few points of interest have been left unsung in this locality.

The fashionable season is over, but there are still many people here, and the stylish landau with its elegant lord and lady is no uncommon sight.

Our plan was to remain at Windermere a couple of days, then move on to Liverpool, but our apartment at the hotel here is so damp and cheerless that we decide to leave for Liverpool to-day, and so the afternoon finds us driving up to the

Adelphi Hotel, and rejoicing in the homelike atmosphere which greets us here.

Thus ends our tour of Ireland, Scotland and the English Lakes. All that now remains is the voyage from here to New York, which we contemplate with glad hearts, for we are longing to set our feet once more upon the dear American soil and feel ourselves surrounded by a loving family and faithful friends. May kind Providence spare us for this anticipated happiness.

After a week of mingled rest and entertainment, the day of our departure is at hand, and what a scene of confusion is the Adelphi Hotel. Passengers for the steamer are taking luncheon, while others move to and fro in an excited way, asking questions or making arrangements with the head porter for the delivery of their baggage. Many carriages stand before the hotel, waiting to convey its guests to the pier; 'buses drive rapidly by filled with travellers, and rows of steamer chairs and trunks crowd each other in the corridors. We reach the Princes Landing in good time, and find our noble ship awaiting the signal to start.

At 2.30 p. m. the usual ringing of gongs and blowing of whistles take place, accompanied by waving handkerchiefs, farewell calls, and kisses wafted across the watery space. And now we are in the middle of the Mersey, steaming on our homeward course.

After the usual programme of settling our belongings, and making final arrangements, we repair to the saloon, where each one entertains himself in the manner that suits him best. The day is not pleasant enough to go on deck, as mist and rain accompany us. The steamer has her full complement of passengers, and we look for a good attendance at dinner this evening, then a gradual falling off for several days.

Thus far our "log" shows a record of weather anything but pleasant. We have had fog, rough sea, rain, and strong head winds, and at this moment the steamer rolls so as to render writing almost impossible. I have never before seen such a seasick-stricken set of voyagers. Only eight of the 320 first cabin passengers respond to the dinner bell, or rather bugle, to-day. The old custom of ringing a gong is superseded by the bugle, which is sounded a half hour before, and at the hour for each meal. For myself, I prefer the gong.

We are all pretty badly shaken up, and feel the effects of the sea generally. To-night is our worst night. The storm rages all night long, and the constant blowing of the fog horn, the racing of the propeller, and the violent beating of the waves against the side of the ship permit little or no sleep. All door-ways are closed, and ventilation is at a low ebb. Many passengers do not retire at all, for various reasons. One says he wishes to be prepared in case of accident. Others are more or less frightened. Some one tells the story of the darkey who preferred a wreck on land to one on sea, because in the first case, one could look about him after the accident, and say, " Well, der yer are." But on the ocean it is more likely to be, " Where are yer?"

I say to a lady at my side that the steamer is "racing frightfully," and she replies: "Dear me! I thought racing was prohibited." And she declares emphatically that she will report the captain on our arrival in New York, for racing in such a sea. When, however, I assure her that in this case " racing " only indicates the speed of the propeller in the storm, her indignation changes to laughter at such nautical ignorance.

This night is really worse than any other in the whole passage. The gale is fiercer, and the ship plunges and tosses incessantly. The doors of the companion-ways are all bolted, and the storm-doors fastened outside. Very few appear at the dinner-table. The old maxim that "he who sleeps, dines," may find itself established here in negatives, as there are neither diners nor sleepers.

To-day is clear and beautiful, and the sea,

towards noon, is smooth. The purser and other officials prophesy that we will be in dock in New York harbor to-morrow between two and three o'clock. The appearance of the pilot on board to-day at noon assures us that we are indeed nearing home. This evening will be a busy one, as the last preparations for leaving the steamer must be made. What a pleasant occupation!

A concert was suggested for the evening, and we were asked, among others, to contribute to the entertainment, but the project falls through, as there are too many conflicting claims upon every one's attention just now.

This forenoon is spent in attending to those innumerable " last things," which can never be done until the last minute. We hope to reach New York at two o'clock. The rain, which comes down in torrents, is a disappointment to the many who have anticipated sitting on deck and enjoying the scenery.

Now we approach the Cunard Docks, upon which are visible innumerable friends of the passengers, with smiling faces, waving handkerchiefs, and other demonstrations of delight. We land at last amid endless joyous greetings. Now there is a scramble for the baggage. Men and women, messenger boys, policemen, Custom House officers, wagons and trunks seem inextricably mingled together. Finally our trunks are found, and to our great relief inspected, and an hour and a half from the time of our arrival we are seated in a railway coach on our way to dear old Philadelphia, our home, and the home of those we love best. And this is the end of one of the happiest tours it has been our good fortune to make.

[THE END.]

www.ingramcontent.com/pod-product-compliance
Lightning Source LLC
Chambersburg PA
CBHW030013240426
43672CB00007B/929